# What
# Auto Mechanics
# Don't Want You to Know

Mark Eskeldson

Technews Publishing

Fair Oaks, CA

D1026462

Library of Congress Catalog Card Number:  98-61089

ISBN:  0-9640560-6-2

Published by
Technews Publishing, a division of Technews Corp.
7840 Madison Avenue, Suite 185, Fair Oaks, CA 95628

FOURTH EDITION

1st Printing

Manufactured in the United States of America.

Cover Design by Paula Schlosser

# DEDICATION

This book is dedicated to the honest and highly skilled auto repair technicians who are tired of dishonest and incompetent mechanics giving their industry a bad name. And to those who lost their jobs because they refused to cheat their customers.

# ABOUT THE AUTHOR

Mark Eskeldson has been involved in the auto repair industry for over 21 years. He has worked as a technician in independent repair shops and new-car dealership service departments, specializing in diagnosis and repair of electrical, driveability and computer problems on late-model cars. Mark was also involved for two years in training mechanics to diagnose and repair computer control systems.

The author hosted "Shop Talk: America's Radio Car Clinic" for four years and is currently certified by ASE (National Institute for Automotive Service Excellence). His books have been featured in *Smart Money, Reader's Digest, Kiplinger's, The Wall Street Journal* and on ABC, NBC and CBS TV.

# ACKNOWLEDGMENTS

This book would not have been possible without the cooperation of many people. My special thanks to the following agencies for the time they gave in interviews, providing documentation for the undercover stories, and for their outstanding work in policing the auto repair facilities of their counties and states:

**ATTORNEYS GENERAL—**
Arizona, California, Florida, Maryland, Minnesota, Missouri, Nevada, New Jersey, New York, Pennsylvania, Tennessee, Texas, Utah, Washington

**CALIFORNIA—**
Bureau of Automotive Repair
Alameda County District Attorney
El Dorado County District Attorney
Sacramento County District Attorney
San Joaquin County District Attorney

**LOUISIANA—**
New Orleans Better Business Bureau

**MICHIGAN—**
Bureau of Automotive Regulation

**NEVADA—**
Department of Consumer Affairs
Washoe County District Attorney

**WISCONSIN—**
Department of Justice

**TV STATIONS—**
KCBS in Los Angeles, CA
KNXV in Phoenix, AZ
KSTP in St. Paul, MN
WJBK in Detroit, MI
WMAQ in Chicago, IL

Thanks also to the National Institute for Automotive Service Excellence (ASE) for their work in certifying technicians, and to the American Automobile Association (AAA) for their Approved Auto Repair program that provides technician training and helps consumers locate reputable auto repair facilities.

# Contents

# Introduction

On the last two big car stories that I covered, I scooped the press by a year or more and had to wait for them to catch up (the Sears auto repair scandal in my first book, and the Ford leasing scandal in *Leasing Lessons*). This time, though, instead of just covering a major automotive story, I was in on it.

Last year, I was contacted by an investigative reporter from KCBS-TV in Los Angeles. He said he was thinking about doing a huge undercover investigation into auto repair rip-offs and asked if I would be willing to help. My contribution: helping him design the investigation so that it would be above reproach. I agreed to help.

In May of 1998, KCBS-TV completed the largest undercover auto repair sting that's been done in the U.S. in over 15 years. The result: Dozens of big-name chain stores were caught selling unnecessary repairs, and some of them were caught charging for services that were never done.

This sting was in the news for at least five days, and the splash it made was so big that it resulted in a hearing at the state capital. Now you can read all about it, starting with "Chain Store Scandals."

Before the KCBS investigation, I already had a mountain of evidence regarding the deceptive business practices of many well-known companies. But the investigation showed that rip-offs were still going on, they were predictable, and they were widespread.

I think it's only fair to say that the dishonest practices that were found at many shops were not always being used by every shop in a particular chain. How do I know that? Because I found workers who were harassed and even fired for refusing to cheat their customers. Some were "team players" and some were not. And therein lies the problem for consumers: In any large chain of repair shops, there are honest and dishonest workers, but how can people tell the difference when the shops all have the same name?

This book was written to give consumers the information they need to avoid being victimized by dishonest or incompetent repair shops. Commonly used tactics from repair scams are exposed, and actual examples are given of well-known shops that have been charged with selling unnecessary parts and services.

Tips are also given for locating well-trained, highly skilled technicians that people can trust. Many vehicle owners spend hundreds (or thousands) of dollars on repairs that aren't necessary, so it's definitely worth the effort to find the most reputable shops.

In this book, you'll learn all about the various "secret warranties" that exist in the repair business, and how they can be used to get free repairs after the "official" warranty expires. Many of my radio listeners have used these tricks to save some serious money on repairs.

And finally, you should expect denials from practically every company I've written about, but don't believe them. The "big-name" companies just wanted to keep their practices a secret, but now you can read about them as I reveal *what all of them didn't want you to know.*

# 1

# Chain Store Scandals;
# Who Can You Trust?

Imagine entering the service area of a shop belonging to a large, well-known auto repair chain and seeing a sign that says, "Warning: Our service advisors have little or no experience or training in automotive repairs, and they are paid a commission on all the repairs they sell. In addition, our mechanics have strict daily quotas, and they are also paid a sales commission on additional repairs and services."

Or how about a more friendly sign saying, "Thank you for bringing your vehicle to Big Name You-Can-Trust-Us Auto Centers. Our employees are participating in a contest to see who can sell the most parts and services, and they would appreciate your cooperation in helping them to win valuable prizes (in addition to keeping their jobs). So buy as many repairs as you can afford, and if you need a higher credit limit on your Big-Name charge card, we can arrange that, too. Because at Big-Name Auto Centers, the customer always comes first."

After seeing signs like that, would you trust them to recommend auto repairs or services? Would anyone trust them? Probably not. And that's exactly why those signs were never posted in the service areas of many large, well-known chain stores even though they were using some (or all) of the very practices I just mentioned. *The companies didn't want you to know.*

### "Dirty Little Secret #1" Slips Out

When undercover cars in California caught Sears Auto Centers selling unnecessary repairs in 1992, the general public was shocked and outraged to learn that the company had quotas, sales commissions, and contests to encourage the sale of additional repairs.

After some said those practices may have caused consumer losses, Sears defended its actions as "common practices in the repair industry," claiming that replacing perfectly good parts before they fail is known as "preventive maintenance."

Most people who heard the excuses made by Sears dismissed them as "PR spin," and the shocking truth of their words went unnoticed—that most (or all) of what they were caught doing really were common practices at many chain stores across the country.

## Quotas, Commissions & Contests

"Big-name" auto repair chains have a long history of using quotas, sales commissions, and contests in their shops. In 1992, after the Sears bust, the New York State Consumer Protection Board conducted a survey of all the major auto repair chains doing business in that state, to find out how many were using sales commissions or bonuses to encourage the sale of additional repairs.

The Board found that almost all of the national chains paid store managers, service writers, and/or mechanics a commission or bonus based on the amount of parts and services they sell. Meineke Muffler said that some of its employees were paid strictly on a commission basis, and Midas Muffler said that its mechanics receive a base salary plus a commission based on the total price of work that is completed. Sears said that its service advisors were paid a straight hourly wage, but I was told that its service advisors still receive a sales commission on tires, shock absorbers and batteries.

Kmart said that its mechanics were paid an hourly wage and were not compensated on a commission or sales basis. The company did not provide any information on other store personnel, but it was later discovered to be using sales quotas, contests, and incentives for managers.

In conclusion, the Board said that consumers have reason for concern when taking their cars to repair shops, because the use of sales incentives increases the chances of consumers being sold unnecessary repairs and people don't usually know which shops are using them.

What kind of sales incentives were used? In the case of Sears, service advisors were paid 3-6% of sales, in addition to their base salary. Some Midas mechanics were paid 13-15% of everything they sold and installed—no hourly wage, just straight commission.

Contests pitting employee against employee, store against store, or zone against zone, were used by Sears, Goodyear, and Kmart. Prizes ranged from an expensive dinner for two (for mechanics) to vacations in Hawaii or Bermuda, and cruises in Alaska or the Caribbean—with cash prizes of $10,000—for managers.

Those types of sales incentives could definitely tempt employees to sell a lot of additional parts and services, whether they're needed or not. *And that's why they tried to keep it a secret.*

### "Dirty Little Secret #2"

The second dirty little secret of chain stores is that they are really "mass merchandisers," not repair shops. That's why they teamed up with the nation's parts manufacturers to start "MAP," the program that was supposed to rebuild consumer confidence and trust in the repair industry after the Sears scandal. And remember those contest prizes (vacation trips and lots of cash)? Those were done (i.e., funded) in cooperation with many large aftermarket manufacturers whose parts were sold by the chains.

The goal of mass merchandisers is to sell as many products as possible. (In other words—sell, sell, sell.) In most industries, this would be a totally ethical and legal business practice. However, when consumers have to rely on repair shops for advice on needed services, and they're not told that employees are being paid (or worse yet, competing) for the sale of additional repairs, this crosses over into the area of deceptive business practices.

Information about the use of commissions, contests and quotas has usually been hidden from the chains' customers. A good example of this was found at Kmart. The company had signs posted in their auto centers titled, "Kmart's Automotive Service Policy" that read, in part:

"Unlike many of its competitors, Kmart does not pay commissions to its service technicians. This policy of professionalism has been in place for more than 15 years, and places Kmart ahead of the industry."

No mention was made of the fact that Kmart mechanics and store managers had quotas, or that contests were being run to encourage the sale of additional parts and services. That information certainly would have been of interest to Kmart's customers, maybe more than what the company said about commissions. *(It was probably just a coincidence that Kmart left that information out,* just like they did in their response to the New York State Consumer Protection Board.)

Withholding material information from consumers, when that information could affect their decision to buy, is a deceptive business practice. (See the "Deceptive Advertising" section later in this chapter.) Of course, the companies will deny that their sales practices have been (or are now) unethical or illegal. *But they didn't want their customers to know about them.*

### Quotas

Quotas of some form or another have been used by most major chain stores, especially the ones that are owned and operated by the parent companies. In the Sears case, auto center workers were found to have a strict daily quota spelling out how many sales of five specific repairs they were required to make for every 8-hour shift they completed. Some employees who failed to meet Sears' quotas were punished by reduced work schedules or transfers to other store departments. (One of their mechanics was transferred to the garden department.)

Documents from lawsuits against Goodyear and

17

Kmart auto centers show that store managers had daily and monthly "sales goals" or "sales objectives" with dire consequences for those who failed to measure up. Memos to store managers referred to the goals with stern reminders that they were to be monitored and followed, and employees who consistently fell short were harassed, intimidated, transferred and/or terminated. *Goals with dire consequences? Sure sounds like quotas to me.*

Goodyear also had "productivity goals" for both mechanics and service associates, and Kmart had them for its mechanics. These "goals" included finding and selling additional repairs, and there were severe consequences for employees who fell short. Goodyear memos listed "minimum productivity" for mechanics as $833 per day at one store and $500 per day at another, with a note to one mechanic that said, "If you cannot meet your objective you will be released from your duties..." A Kmart memo listed their goal per worker at $60 per hour, when their labor rate was only $30-32 per hour.

Goodyear's memo referring to quotas for mechanics (I'm sorry, I mean "productivity objectives") was dated one month after the company made a public announcement about ending the payment of commissions to its mechanics for selling parts and services. At that time, Goodyear Chairman Stanley Gault said, "Sales incentives have been an accepted practice for a wide range of businesses...However, when commissions in auto repair were determined to erode consumer trust, it was time to change the way Goodyear does business."

Incidentally, Goodyear waited until four months after its second state investigation (accusing the company of fraud in its auto centers) to announce that it would discontinue commission-based pay for mechanics working in 900 company-owned stores. No mention was made by Mr. Gault of using (or ending) quotas. Another company memo referred to daily sales quotas (I mean "objectives") almost two months after Goodyear's announcement on commissions.

What makes quotas harmful to consumers is the fact that they require massive sales of additional parts to meet objectives. A Kmart memo to district managers said, "Our gross percent is a result of what we sell—not what the customer asks for." Another Kmart memo to district managers and service managers said, "Average dollars per invoice show lack of add on sales, only selling what the customer originally came in for—nothing more. WE NEED MORE!!"

Free inspections and low-priced services advertised by the chains rarely (if ever) generate enough revenue to meet quotas, and their hourly labor rates aren't high enough to make up for insufficient sales. Because of this, most (if not all) of these companies would rather see their mechanics installing lots of high-priced parts than simply diagnosing and repairing problems, collecting only their hourly labor rate. (Don't forget, they're "mass merchandisers.")

The bottom line is that quotas often turn mechanics and service writers into aggressive salespeople, with so much pressure to produce that consumers would be wise to question any repair recommendations that are made. *And that's why they didn't want you to know.*

### Deceptive Advertising

False (or deceptive) advertising is a dishonest, illegal practice that is defined by the FTC Act as "misleading in a material respect." One state's Consumer Protection Act says that "failure to state a material fact if the failure deceives or tends to deceive" is a deceptive trade practice.

According to those legal definitions, false or deceptive advertising has been commonly used by many well-known auto centers, especially in the area of brake services. Low-priced brake ads that say "Brake Reline (most cars)" or "Brake Service (most cars)" are almost always deceptive.

The average brake job at major repair chains runs between $160 and $200, so the companies know that "most cars" are not going to get a brake job for $59 or $69. Plus, most people will have to pay extra for semi-metallic pads, since those are required on about 90% of the cars on the road.

In fact, the Pennsylvania Attorney General charged Sears in 1992 with violating the state's Unfair Trade Practices and Consumer Protection Law by using deceptive advertising to promote a sale on disc brakes. Although Sears' ads had a small-print note that said, "semi-metallic material and imports extra," the attorney general said that Sears' ad implied that the company would do brake relines on "most" vehicles for $48.

Since the advertised price would not apply to about 90% of the cars on the road, the attorney general said the ads were deceptive. To settle the charges, Sears paid $4,000 to the state and agreed to refund the extra $20 that was charged to 219 customers.

Documents from the Kmart lawsuit show that the company was running low-priced brake ads with the intention of selling more expensive brake services. A "Kmart Brake Facts" sheet that was given to workers said, "Rebuilding wheel cylinders is a mandatory part of our brake service. Rebuilding calipers should be recommended to every brake customer..." However, Kmart's low-priced brake ads said, "most cars" and "no hidden costs," even though the wheel cylinders and calipers that workers were instructed to sell (to everyone) were not included in their advertised brake prices.

At Goodyear, a former service manager said that he was told by the company's training instructor and the district manager that stores were supposed to be selling major brake overhauls on all of the vehicles that came in for ordinary brake service.

Have you noticed that Midas Muffler & Brake has stopped advertising brake prices, other than their long-running radio ad that says, "For a limited time, get 25% off brake pads and shoes at participating Midas shops"? The company was forced to change its advertising practices in early 1994 after an investigation by the New York Attorney General's office.

Midas had been advertising brake services for $59 to $69 and new mufflers for $24.95, with a disclaimer that additional parts were often needed at substantial extra cost. (Boy, was that an understatement.) The investigation found that only 5% of Midas' customers got a muffler for the advertised price. In fact, 95% of consumers who went to their shops for the $24.95 muffler paid, on average, over four times the advertised price. On brake jobs, 88% of consumers who went to their shops for the $59 or $69 brake service ended up paying more than three-and-a-half times the advertised price. *Now that's the "Midas touch."*

According to the attorney general, "These ads were mere come-ons designed to lure consumers into the repair shop where they were hit with unexpectedly high repair bills. When only five percent of consumers pay the actual advertised price, that price is essentially a fantasy and should not be advertised as real."

Under the terms of a settlement agreed to by Midas, the company will not advertise a specific price for an auto repair service unless at least 65% of those who purchase the advertised repair do not purchase additional parts or services to complete the repair at a total cost in excess of

15% above the advertised price.

One year after the New York settlement, Midas was running radio ads for mufflers—with no prices. In their new ads, Midas was taking shots at competitors by saying, "There are many places that advertise really low prices on mufflers and exhaust systems just to try to get you in the door." So after eight-plus years of running their own low-priced, deceptive, bait-and-switch ads, Midas was attacking competitors for doing the same thing.

That 1994 settlement seems to have ended large-scale price advertising by Midas. (It's hard to imagine them running ads for $200 brake jobs.) So now the company runs "warm & fuzzy" ads aimed at women, offering discounts on infant car seats and telling stories about customers baking cookies for "those nice people at Midas."

**Bait-and-Switch Scams**

"Bait and switch" is a type of dishonest, illegal business practice that involves running an ad for one product or service with no intention of selling it at the advertised price. Instead, the plan is to sell another, more-expensive product or service to customers who come in for the advertised item. This practice is commonly used in many areas of the auto repair business, especially in the sale of tires, brakes, mufflers and tune-ups. Bait-and-switch scams usually fall under the category of false or deceptive advertising. (See the previous section.)

**Overcharges**

This little trick can bring in a lot of extra money for a major repair company: overcharging a little on many items. If it's done right, it can be made to look like an innocent mistake, and when an overcharge is discovered, all the shop has to do is act apologetic and immediately refund the money. They can even blame it on "computer error."

In November of 1991, Kmart Auto Centers agreed to refund $63,994 to Agency Rent-A-Car for overcharges on brake parts that Agency had discovered during its own audit. The rental car company was one of Kmart's many national fleet customers that were promised discount prices on brake services.

Documents from the Kmart lawsuit show that the company's own internal audit in 1992 found 26% of its automotive customers being charged higher than manufacturer's list prices on parts that were purchased locally. A similar audit in 1993 found that 21% of Kmart's automotive customers were again charged more than list prices in the stores that were audited.

List prices are the regular prices that are charged by most shops in the repair business, including the ones who don't even pretend to offer low prices. Charging customers more than list was against Kmart's "official" company policy on being the "low-cost leader" in the auto repair industry, and obviously contradicted Kmart's ads for auto repair that said, "No hidden costs." (Well, it is really hard to make a profit—or meet a quota—when all a shop gets is customers who are responding to cheap ads.)

Once again, in 1993, Kmart was accused of overcharging customers over a 5-year period, but this time the charges involved its California retail stores. A statewide investigation found "price-scanner overcharging" on sale items at 72 Kmart stores.

In one county, investigators "shopped" at 10 Kmart stores. At all 10 stores, investigators were overcharged (not given the advertised price) on one out of four purchases. (What a coincidence—overcharges on 25% of certain purchases! And the overcharge number from Kmart's own 1992 auto repair audit was 26%!)

As a result of their investigation, the San Diego City Attorney charged Kmart with unfair competition and false advertising. Kmart agreed to pay $985,000 to settle the charges, and its stores in San Diego County were put on criminal probation.

## Phantom Sales

"Phantom sales" refers to charges for parts, services or repairs that were not provided. This practice has been found in a number of shops that belong to major chains, as documented in lawsuits and undercover investigations. (It's also been found in some dealership service departments, as part of a "scheduled maintenance" scam.)

For example, in a recent investigation involving three Montgomery Ward Auto Express stores in California, undercover agents were charged for alignments on six visits, but only one alignment was done. Two recent undercover investigations of Econo Lube N' Tune shops in California and Nevada found shops charging for repairs and/or services that were not done. Econo Lube agreed to pay $284,000 to settle the California charges that also included recommending unnecessary repairs.

## The Lifetime Guarantee Scam

"Lifetime guarantees" are sometimes used in chain stores that do brakes, mufflers, alignments, or transmissions. These are almost always a bad deal for consumers, who pay higher prices for the initial repair with the mistaken belief that they will save money in the long run. But they probably won't. If the original muffler lasted 80-90,000 miles, the second one will probably last longer than the rest of the car. So why pay extra for a lifetime guarantee? (Especially when it might be worthless.)

Think about it: Why would a repair shop—that's in business to make money—want to do a lot of repairs for free? They don't plan to. They plan on selling additional (usually high-priced) parts and services to most of the people who come back. And they're often quick to refuse warranty work to customers who won't buy additional repairs. They just make up an excuse that sounds good, like: "Your disc pads do have a lifetime guarantee, but they wore out because your calipers and (insert more high-priced parts here) are bad, so I can't warranty your brakes without first replacing the (expensive parts)."

Chain stores frequently use the lifetime guarantee scam to sell additional, unnecessary repairs during the initial service. When shop personnel can't find any legitimate parts that need replacing, they can always say, "Those parts haven't failed yet, but we can't guarantee your brake job without replacing them." The implication is that it's not safe to leave those parts on the car, when they might actually work fine for another 4 or 5 years. (Of course, they neglect to mention that.) This scam is also used on customers who refuse to buy additional parts after being told that the parts are bad.

**The Free Inspection Scam**

Offers of "free brake inspections" or "free safety inspections" should be eyed with suspicion, especially if the company spent a lot of money to advertise them. In most cases, these are offered by companies that have sales commissions, contests and/or quotas that put serious pressure on employees to sell expensive repairs. (They have to pay for all those ads, you know.) In the past, some of the biggest repair scams involved using this trick to find new victims.

A variation on the free inspection scam is used on

consumers who go to a shop with a specific problem that they want diagnosed and repaired, but they don't know what their car needs. When the service advisor is told the symptoms, he says, "Sure, we can find out what's wrong. Now, Mrs. Smith, would you like us to perform a free safety inspection while your car is here?" Chances are the shop will do an inspection anyway, whether the customer wants it or not, because they want to find other stuff to sell—hopefully for some serious money. (Once again, that's why chain stores are called "mass merchandisers.")

If the customer is lucky, the shop might actually figure out what caused the original complaint, but the problem better show up fast. Chain stores are not in business to just collect their hourly labor charge—they need to sell a lot of parts to meet their sales quotas, so they can't spend a lot of time on one car. This is why a lot of people have spent significant amounts of money on various repairs at these stores, and left with the original problem still needing repair.

To avoid this, always insist on the symptoms being written on your original estimate (for example, "diagnose brake noise" or "diagnose poor acceleration"). That way, if your car isn't fixed after you've been sold parts and/or services, you'll then have the evidence needed to prove that you were sold unnecessary repairs.

## Inexperience and/or Incompetence

Chain stores spend huge amounts of money on advertising to convince the public that they really are experts who can be trusted to service and repair cars. In some cases, that may be true. However, in far too many cases, their service advisors and managers have so little training and/ or experience that consumers should not rely on them for professional advice.

A 1992 investigation of auto repair practices by the New York Attorney General's office revealed the widespread employment of service advisors with little or no previous training or experience in auto repair. In spite of their obvious lack of qualifications, their job description included inspecting and diagnosing vehicles prior to making service and repair recommendations to consumers. According to the attorney general, those practices were not limited to auto centers in New York, but were being used nationwide.

Franchises make up a large part of the repair chains, and their "expertise" requirement for owners or managers is often nonexistent. Ads that offer auto repair franchises to the public frequently say, "No automotive experience is necessary." (Just the $50,000 to $100,000 franchise fee.) No problem, you might be thinking, the companies will provide the training. *And that's the problem.*

A major repair company that offers franchises is going to make most of its money on the monthly royalties each shop is required to pay to the corporation. (This is typically 7-10% of the monthly gross sales, but it can be a lot higher in some cases.) Obviously, the company has a major financial incentive to encourage its franchisees to sell as much as possible. If new owners or managers have no previous experience, it's a lot easier to teach them how to sell expensive unnecessary repairs because they don't know any better—until they get busted.

In a consumer-protection lawsuit against Cottman Transmission Systems (a franchisor) filed by the Maryland Attorney General, a former manager testified that Cottman did not require any mechanics experience to be a center manager. He said, "Their position was that you were better off without mechanics experience." He also testified that he went through three weeks of training at the Cottman center, and no time was spent on technical training—it was all spent on sales.

Cottman trainees were required to memorize sales tracts before class, and most of the class time was spent on role playing, salesman vs. customer. The emphasis was on how to get cars into the shop without giving customers any prices for major repairs until their vehicles were disassembled, for the purpose of selling them complete transmission overhauls.

The trial court found that Cottman required its franchises to use procedures that result in the sale of unnecessary repairs, ruled that Cottman was guilty of a deceptive trade practice, and fined the company $100,000. A higher court later ordered the company to make restitution to consumers who were victimized.

Incidentally, a number of Cottman Transmission franchises have been charged with fraudulent business practices following undercover investigations in 3 states. And the company is still offering transmission franchises for people with "$35,000 Minimum cash required." One of their ads said, "Cottman Transmission...America's most respected name in transmission repair..." (Compared to ?)

## Class-Action Lawsuits: Kmart & Goodyear

Both Kmart and Goodyear were targeted by class-action lawsuits (in 1993-94) over allegations of fraud in their auto centers. The companies were both accused of: using incentive/quota systems that encouraged the sale of unnecessary repairs; false and misleading advertising; and making false/misleading statements and material omissions to its customers.

Kmart got its lawsuit dismissed in two states on jurisdictional issues, but it was recently filed again in Louisiana. In 1997, the Goodyear lawsuit was settled after the company agreed to pay $70 million.

**Investigations & Class-Action Lawsuits**

Most of the biggest names in the auto repair business have been accused of fraudulent business practices in their shops after undercover investigations were done. Many of the practices outlined in this chapter were believed responsible for activities that got the companies in trouble. The following list shows which well-known companies were targeted by state investigations and/or class-action lawsuits, as well as the (known) amounts of settlements that were obtained.

Aamco Transmissions ($600,000 + restitution)
Big O Tires ($172,000)
Cottman Transmissions ($160,000+)
Econo Lube N' Tune ($285,000+)
Firestone ($350,000+)
Goodyear ($70 million+)
Kmart
Lee Myles Transmissions
Midas Muffler ($700,000+)
Montgomery Ward ($1 million+)
Parnelli Jones/Dobbs Tire ($800,000)
Purrfect Auto Service
Quality Tune-up ($2 million)
Sears ($48 million+)
Tire Pro ($55,000)
Winston Tire ($1.5 million)

For Sears, settlements of investigations and class-action lawsuits from their 1992 bust is believed to have cost the company over $48 million. (They had agreed to make restitution to 900,000 customers who were allegedly sold unnecessary repairs.) And Aamco Transmissions has the dubious honor of being the only auto repair company to be accused of fraud by 14 states that were conducting investigations at the same time.

## 1998—Chain Stores Caught in Huge Sting

In May of 1998, KCBS-TV in Los Angeles completed the largest undercover auto repair sting that's been done in the U.S. in over a decade. Using hidden cameras and specially prepared vehicles, their operatives made over 90 undercover runs at shops throughout Southern California. The results of their investigation: Dozens of big-name chain stores were caught recommending and/or selling unnecessary repairs, and some were caught charging for repairs that weren't even done.

Here are the chain store results: According to KCBS, shops from the following chains were caught trying to rip off their investigators. (The numbers represent the percentage of visits that involved attempted rip-offs.) Tune-up Masters (80%), Montgomery Ward Auto Express (60%), Purrfect Auto Centers (60%), Midas Muffler & Brake Shops (40%), Econo Lube N' Tune (40%), and Kmart/Penske Auto Centers (20%). The average for attempted rip-offs at all chain stores (that were visited) was 50%.

A few independent shops were also caught in the sting, but their numbers (and offenses) were minor compared to what was found at the chains. Only 2 out of 10 independents that were visited tried to sell unnecessary repairs.

The results of the KCBS investigation were initially broadcast over a three-day period, then several follow-up shows were done over the next two months. One follow-up story showed what happened when undercover cars were sent back to some of the same shops that were stung the first time: Some of them were caught again (Purrfect

Auto Service and Tuneup Masters).

For more details on this investigation, be sure to visit the "CarInfo.com" Web site (www.carinfo.com) on the Internet. Look for "Auto Repair Secrets." (If KCBS still has the whole story online, you'll find a link there.) This Web site also has lots of information on rip-offs in the new-car buying and leasing business.

**Survey: Chain Stores & Customer Satisfaction**

In the September, 1994 issue of *Consumer Reports,* the results of their Annual Questionnaire were published after analyzing 40,000 readers' experiences with repair shops between 1991 and 1993. To arrive at an overall satisfaction rating, shops were graded on median prices, repeat problems with the repair, pressure to sell additional parts, and whether the job was completed on time.

Out of 22,000 responses from readers whose cars had brake repairs, independent repair shops came in first in overall customer satisfaction, with a median brake price of $150. Dealership service departments came in second, with a median brake price of $200.

Major chain stores scored much lower in overall customer satisfaction, due to more sales pressure, repeat problems, and jobs not completed when promised. Meineke Muffler came in 4th ($150), Midas Muffler came in 5th ($180), Goodyear Auto Service: 6th ($170), Firestone Mastercare Service Centers: 7th ($180), and Sears Auto Centers: 8th (last place) with a median brake price of $200.

Similar results were seen in the responses from 12,000 readers whose cars had muffler repairs. Again, independent repair shops came in first, dealership service departments came in second, and major chain stores came in 5th through 9th.

## Chain Store Advertising & Customer Loyalty

One can't help but notice that chain stores do an awful lot of advertising. As a matter of fact, most of them spend at least 5-10% of their gross revenue on advertising, a figure that is 5-10 times the amount spent by most independent repair shops. Why the big difference? I believe the answer lies in customer satisfaction and loyalty, which is noticeably lower for chains than it is for independents, as shown by the *Consumer Reports* survey.

Lower customer satisfaction causes less repeat business and fewer recommendations to friends, requiring a business to increase its advertising to find new customers. (Simply put, the more people they burn, the more they need to replace.)

Independent repair shops don't have millions of dollars to spend on advertising, so they can't afford to find a lot of new customers on a regular basis. By treating people honestly and fairly, they can generate higher customer satisfaction and tremendous loyalty. The result: greater repeat business and, of course, free referrals from their customers—*the type of advertising that money can't buy.*

# WHO CAN YOU TRUST?

As the *Consumer Reports* survey showed, independent repair shops usually have the most satisfied customers. So, if you want to find a shop you can trust, ignore all the advertising and do some research. There are shops out there that are honest and professional, but you have to look hard to find them. (For more information, see Chapter 15: "Finding Mechanics You Can Trust.")

# 2

# Brake Bandits & Brake Jobs

You've probably seen ads for $59 or $69 brake relines, realizing that most shops charge over twice that amount. Why do you think some shops charge so much less? Because they're "nice guys" and the other shops are just greedy? Or is there a catch?

There's a catch: Few people actually get their brakes done for only $59 or $69. It's fairly common for a customer to receive a revised estimate of $200, $300, or more after bringing a vehicle in for a low-priced brake service. I've seen many brake jobs (at chain stores) that cost $300 to $400, and even some for $1200 to $1800. ($1800! Sounds like someone's boat payment was due.)

There's not much profit on a $59 or $69 brake reline, so when you see one of those ads, it's a safe bet that someone plans on selling a lot of high-priced additional repairs to the people who come in for the advertised service. (In fact, an investigation of Midas Muffler and Brake Shops found that 88% of their brake customers ended up paying over three-and-a-half times the advertised price.)

How do these shops convince so many people that they need $300 or $400 brake jobs, especially after they came in for the $59 special? They use scare tactics.

Brake shops probably have more potential for consumer fraud than any other type of repair shop. For most drivers, a vehicle that runs rough or makes noise is irritating, but a vehicle without brakes is absolutely frightening. Many unethical shops have taken advantage of this fear, using scare tactics to sell unnecessary (and usually high-priced) brake repairs.

Shops that use dishonest "bait and switch" tactics know that there are plenty of people who will go to an unfamiliar shop for repairs if they think that shop has the lowest prices in town. They also know that there are plenty of people who think they can get something for nothing (like a "free" inspection).

How does a dishonest shop find enough customers to stay in business and make piles of money? All they have to do is offer free brake inspections or cheap brake relines, and they will have what seems to be an endless supply of victims. The following story is a typical example of how shops use free inspections and low-priced brake relines to attract a lot of people, and then try to sell them high-priced repairs.

One day, I received a call at the shop from one of our customers. She had taken her car to a well-known chain store for their advertised "free brake inspection." They told her that her brakes were in pretty bad shape and that it would cost about $500 to repair them.

She had called us to ask if we thought that was too much money to pay for a brake job. I told her that price was pretty high, and that if her brakes really were in such bad shape, someone would have noticed. So I pulled her repair orders from our files to see if any notations had been made about her brakes.

We had done a routine service about two months prior to that and had inspected her brakes at that time. The notes on the repair order stated that the brakes were in good shape, with about 80% of the brake lining remaining (her brakes should have lasted at least another 20,000 to 25,000 miles). The drums, calipers, and wheel cylinders were all in good condition when we inspected them.

When I read the notes to her, she said she didn't understand why they were telling her that her brakes were so bad when we had just said they were all right. I said it looked like they were trying to sell her repairs that weren't needed, and told her that she should not allow them to do any work on her car. I also recommended that she file a complaint against that shop with the Bureau of Automotive Repair. (That shop was busted later on.)

That was not an isolated incident; many shops have had similar experiences with people who were tempted by ads for free inspections and low-priced brake services at well-known chain stores.

In the past, many of these shops advertised free brake inspections, but the public must have figured out that it was just a scheme to sell brake repairs, so now they offer "free safety inspections" instead. This also gives shops an opportunity to sell other (sometimes unnecessary) repairs and/or services.

Most shops that advertise low-priced brake relines or free inspections pay their mechanics a commission on sales in addition to a small salary. The salary is usually only 40-50% of the going rate for a good mechanic, so their mechanics have to sell a lot of additional repairs just to earn a living.

This practice of paying mechanics a sales commission (instead of a decent wage) encourages the sale of unnecessary repairs, especially when business is slow or there is a lack of willing customers who really need additional repairs. If business slows down for a while, a mechanic who doesn't sell unnecessary repairs may not make enough money to live on.

Most of the mechanics who go to work for the low-priced brake shops are not well-trained, highly skilled technicians. They're what's known in the industry as "parts changers," which is a name given to less-skilled mechanics who replace a lot of parts, instead of diagnosing and repairing only the defective items.

This explains why they are willing to work for a low salary plus commission. If they were highly skilled, they could easily get a job somewhere else at a considerably higher salary, without having to sell any additional repairs.

Since these mechanics are not usually well-trained, it's easier to convince them that they're doing customers a favor by replacing parts that don't look bad. They're often told by management that certain parts should be replaced to prevent future problems, and training programs that are run by the company (or by parts suppliers) are usually geared toward selling more parts.

The most common scams in the brake business involve the use of free inspections, quotas, sales contests and commissions, deceptive advertising, bait and switch, lifetime warranties, and the latest fraudulent sales tactic: telling customers that their brake fluid is contaminated so all the expensive parts have to be replaced.

## MIDAS MUFFLER & BRAKE SHOPS
### Undercover Investigations

**1998.** Four Midas Muffler & Brake Shops were caught recommending unnecessary repairs in a huge undercover investigation that was done by KCBS-TV in Southern California. One example: According to KCBS, a Midas shop tried to sell their investigators front and rear brakes, plus a transmission service (total: $529), when none of those repairs were needed. (Dozens of other chain stores were also caught in this sting. See Chapter 1 for more details.)

**1996-97.** The Bureau of Automotive Repair charged four Midas Muffler & Brake Shops with selling unnecessary repairs after undercover investigations confirmed the offenses. All four shops were given temporary license suspensions that required the shops to close. The three shops in Southern California were closed for 10 days, the shop in Northern California for 6 days.

**1994.** The New York State Attorney General forced Midas to change its advertising practices after an investigation found that 88% of Midas' brake customers were paying over three-and-a-half times the advertised price. (See Chapter 1, "Deceptive Advertising" for more details.)

**1992-93.** Charges of deceptive business practices were filed by the Pennsylvania Attorney General against 12 Midas Muffler & Brake Shops in the Pittsburgh area following an undercover investigation. In a joint operation between the city police, state police, and the state Bureau of Consumer Protection, a female detective posing as a consumer visited 10 Midas shops selected at random from the phone book.

Driving a car that was previously inspected under the supervision of the State Police, the detective went to the shops and requested a state inspection or safety check. Three of the shops were charged with issuing inspection certificates after failing to detect repairs needed to bring the vehicle into compliance with state inspection requirements.

All of the shops visited were charged with failing to note serious safety defects, and some with recommending unnecessary repairs. In addition to the 10 shops, two others were charged with recommending hundreds of dollars worth of unnecessary brake repairs after consumer complaints were filed with the state.

The 12 Midas franchises settled the case after agreeing to pay the state $51,250 for the costs of the investigation and to resolve the consumer complaints by providing refunds or additional repairs at no charge. They also promised to "work in good faith" with the state to settle any outstanding complaints.

In an unrelated 1992 Philadelphia investigation, four company-owned Midas shops were visited by state undercover cars. One of the shops was charged with recommending $452 in unnecessary repairs; the other three did not recommend any repairs that weren't needed. To settle the charges, Midas agreed to pay $10,000 in penalties and costs of the investigation.

**1989.** After several undercover investigations by the California Bureau of Automotive Repair, nine more Midas shops were charged with fraudulent business practices for recommending and/or selling unnecessary repairs, in violation of the 1986 court order. Most of the shops were put on probation for three years.

**1986.** After receiving numerous consumer complaints, the California Bureau of Automotive Repair and district attorney's offices from four counties started an undercover investigation of nine Midas Muffler & Brake Shops. The shops were all individually owned franchises, and were located in four counties.

A 15-month investigation (ending in 1986) resulted in the Midas shops being charged in civil complaints with fraudulent business practices. The charges included making "false and misleading statements in order to sell automotive services, parts, and repairs," charging customers more than the estimated price, performing repairs "in an incompetent manner," and recommending repairs that were not needed.

The shops were also charged with offering free safety checks to get people to bring in their cars, then after the cars were up on a hoist and inoperative, mechanics would say that repairs were needed, even if they weren't.

Undercover vehicles with practically all new brake parts were taken to the shops. (For example, some vehicles had worn-out brake shoes, but all other brake parts were new.) According to the Bureau, investigators posing as customers documented the sale of unnecessary repairs; some of the brake parts that were replaced were brand new, with less than 50 miles on them.

A deputy district attorney who worked on the case claimed that the Midas shops used scare tactics that were designed to close the sale, leading customers to believe that brake failure was so imminent that they shouldn't drive their car to another shop for a lower price or a second opinion. In what he claimed was an example of practices at the shops, a woman who had taken her car to one of the shops for brake work was given a worksheet that said her brake master cylinder was "ready to blow."

The Midas shops were also charged with routinely selling new coil springs that were not needed. One of the deputy district attorneys stated that the shops tried to sell new springs to practically all consumers who brought in certain General Motors vehicles. (Similar charges were made against a large Midas shop in Michigan.)

To settle the case, Midas International agreed to pay a civil judgment of $100,000 and the individual shops agreed to pay an additional $400,000. (This settlement also involved muffler advertising and repairs. See Chapter 5, "Muffler Shops," for more details.) A permanent injunction was entered against all Midas Muffler & Brake Shops in California, prohibiting the sale of unnecessary parts and repairs.

## MIDAS MUFFLER & BRAKE SHOPS, GOODYEAR AUTO SERVICE CENTER, AVELLINO'S TIRE & AUTO SERVICE CENTER
### Undercover Investigation, Pennsylvania

**1989.** The state Bureau of Consumer Protection had received numerous complaints about the sale of unnecessary brake repairs, so an undercover investigation was set up to go "shopping" at 35 auto repair centers in southeastern Pennsylvania. The Bureau shopped not only at repair centers that had generated complaints, but at others as well.

Undercover cars were prepared by the Keystone AAA Diagnostic Center so the brakes were in good working condition; some vehicles had all new brakes. Minor problems were then created immediately before the vehicles were taken to the repair shops.

In some cases, the wear indicators on new disc brake pads were intentionally bent, causing the front brakes to squeal. Investigators claim that they were sold new disc pads to cure the problem, when all that was needed was to bend the wear indicators so they didn't touch the rotors. In other cases, air was pumped into a brake line, causing a low brake pedal. Investigators said they were sold new master cylinders when all that was needed to cure the problem was to bleed the air out of the system.

As a result of the investigation, four Midas Muffler & Brake Shops, two Avellino's Tire & Auto Service Centers, and one Goodyear Tire Center were accused of recommending or performing unnecessary brake repairs. The Bureau claimed that each shop tried to sell unnecessary repairs on two or three occasions. One of the Midas shops was owned by the parent company, Midas International; the other three were franchises. The Goodyear store was also owned by its parent company, Goodyear Tire & Rubber Co.

To settle the charges, the operators of the four Midas shops agreed to pay total civil penalties of $7,000; the operator of Avellino's $2,700; and Goodyear $2,500. They also promised not to violate state law or to "knowingly misrepresent that services, replacements, or repairs are needed if they are not needed."

## A WORD OF ADVICE

When your vehicle needs brake work, find a reputable, highly skilled technician. His estimate may seem higher than some shops because he uses higher quality parts than they do. It may also seem higher because he's giving you an honest estimate, with no hidden surprises, and the other shops aren't. Shopping around for the lowest price will only increase your chances of being ripped off.

*What Auto Mechanics Don't Want You to Know*

# 3

# Tire & Auto Centers

Like department store auto centers, many tire and auto centers were designed to offer "one-stop shopping for all your automotive needs." In addition to the basic tire store menu, many of the larger stores offer tune-ups, air conditioning, cooling system services, batteries and some electrical repairs.

Millions of customers have been attracted by the big names of these companies, feeling confident that they would receive honest and professional service. (Those massive advertising campaigns probably helped, too.) While some stores may have offered honest and competent service, too many adopted the idea of "one-stop looting for all their financial needs."

## Advertising Low-Priced Services

Millions of dollars have been spent by these shops to advertise low-priced tires and other services, using TV, radio, newspapers and even free "valuable discount" coupon books that arrived in mailboxes across the country. Free brake or safety inspections, low-priced tires, cheap brake jobs, air conditioning specials, cooling system services, etc.—ads for everything imaginable have been used to get people into their shops. And the ads worked. Millions of people did go in for tires and services because of the ads, thinking that they were going to save money. But in too many cases, instead of saving money, they were ripped off.

## Deceptive Advertising

Low-priced ads are often run by many tire and auto stores with the intention of selling expensive additional repairs to those who come in from the ads. In many cases, those ads are deceptive because their workers receive training on how to "upsell" as many customers as possible. Of course, the workers receive "incentives" for every successful sale. (I call these "incentives to steal.")

Sometimes, sloppy repairs are done on vehicles when the owner refuses to buy expensive, additional parts and/ or services. In the case of alignments, workers might only do a "set-the-toe-and-let-it-go," which is basically only a third of a proper alignment. Worse yet, customers may be charged for alignments that aren't even done. (These are known as phantom sales, and they have been confirmed in many undercover investigations.)

## Sales Commissions and Contests

Many tire and auto shops have paid their employees a sales commission or bonus for parts and services that were sold to customers. This has been a common practice in the repair business, and it was confirmed by CEOs from Sears and Goodyear after their shops were stung by undercover investigations.

Training sessions, pep talks, contests and prizes for the most sales were often used to motivate employees to sell as much as possible. But those practices encouraged the sale of unnecessary parts and services, and caused many shops to get busted.

## Quotas

The term "quota" has taken on such a negative meaning that most (if not all) of the major repair companies deny having (or ever using) quotas. They usually admit to having "goals" or "objectives" that have consequences for those who fall short, though. Those are really quotas, and they have been—and still are—quite common.

Quotas are commonly used for mechanics (the companies call these "productivity goals") and for store managers, where they are referred to as "sales goals" or "sales objectives." The latter quotas are also used for district or regional managers, and apply to their whole territory.

Sales or productivity quotas can cause so much pressure to be put on employees that they are tempted (or forced) to sell a lot of unnecessary repairs just to keep their jobs. While some have refused—and been fired, others have gone along until their consciences wouldn't allow it anymore. (And the ones who were never bothered by the rip-offs were often promoted for being good "team players.")

## Free Inspections, Cheap Oil Changes, Lifetime Alignments & Other Scams

Tire and auto centers often use free inspections and other "valuable services" (like cheap oil changes) to attract new customers. *Don't fall for these tricks.* They usually indicate that a shop is using commissions and/or quotas, or that they're desperate for new customers. (What happened to all their old customers? Why isn't the shop getting a lot of new customers from referrals?)

Some of these shops offer "lifetime alignments," with a promise that "you'll never have to pay for another one as long as you own your car." Don't fall for this either; it's usually a scam. The shops get higher prices for the first alignment, then when people come back later for a free one, they just find something else to sell them, whether it's really needed or not. (It's in the fine print of their guarantee: "Additional repairs may be needed to restore the suspension to proper operation before it can be aligned.")

## Scare Tactics

Unscrupulous mechanics and salesmen sometimes use scare tactics to sell additional parts and repairs, especially with female customers. They might say that a wheel could fall off or the steering could go out if certain parts aren't replaced. *Don't fall for this trick.* It is extremely rare for a wheel to fall off, or steering to go out, without any warning.

A front end part that is bad enough to cause total steering loss will usually have other symptoms for weeks before it finally breaks. A vibration or shimmy in the front end; sloppy or erratic steering; or squeaking, grinding, or clunking noises should be checked as soon as possible to make sure the vehicle is safe to drive.

Scare tactics (and other tricks mentioned in this book) have been widely used to sell lots of additional repairs, whether they were needed or not. And most of the big tire and auto companies have been caught doing just that.

## FIRESTONE AUTO CENTERS
### Undercover Investigations

**1996.** A hidden-camera investigation by KSTP-TV in St. Paul (MN) caught 4 out of 6 Firestone stores recommending and/or selling unnecessary repairs. The station's undercover car was thoroughly serviced and checked by several experts, then it was sent to area Firestone stores where the driver asked for a complete inspection.

Two of the Firestone stores said that the car did not need any repairs. But the other four recommended over $1,000 in repairs, including new hoses, filters and fluid changes, even though those things had just been done. One store tried to sell new struts that KSTP's experts said were not needed.

**1995.** A Firestone store in Merced (CA) was charged with selling unnecessary repairs after 3 undercover runs by the Bureau of Automotive Repair confirmed the offenses. Over $1,200 in unnecessary brake repairs were sold to undercover agents. To settle the charges, the shop paid $18,900 and agreed to a 90-day suspension.

**1993.** A Firestone store in Visalia (CA) was charged with selling unnecessary repairs and charging for repairs that were not done. Three undercover runs by the Bureau of Automotive Repair confirmed the offenses, then investigators found over 200 violations. To settle the charges, Firestone agreed to pay $169,500. The store was closed.

Other investigations have also resulted in charges of selling unnecessary repairs at Firestone stores:

1998—Portland, OR: $17,500 penalty; 1 store
1992—West Bloomfield, MI: $1,150 penalty; 1 store
1984—Ventura Co., CA: $150,000 settlement; 1 store

## GOODYEAR AUTO CENTERS
### Class-Action Lawsuit

**1994.** In October, a class-action lawsuit was filed against Goodyear Tire and Rubber Company alleging fraudulent business practices in its auto centers. The company was accused of using quotas, sales commissions, and contests that resulted in the sale of unnecessary repairs. The lawsuit was settled for $70 million in 1997. (See Chapter 1, "Chain Store Scandals," for more information.)

## GOODYEAR AUTO CENTERS
### Undercover Investigations

**1994-95.** Investigations conducted by the California Bureau of Automotive Repair resulted in 8 Goodyear Auto Centers being charged with fraudulent business practices. Undercover runs documented the sale of unnecessary repairs at the shops. All 8 were franchises.

**1994.** On October 14, *ABC News 20/20* aired a show featuring their undercover investigation into a number of company-owned Goodyear Auto Centers in several states. *20/20* had senior New York State Motor Vehicle inspectors prepare their undercover car to make sure it was in top running condition. The car received a tune-up, new spark plugs, wires, and struts, etc., at a total cost of $2,000.

At one shop, their female reporter was sold $300 in repairs that *20/20* said were unnecessary, including new struts, fuel filter, and a transmission service.

At another shop, their undercover car was sent in with

a disconnected fuel injector plug (to create a rough-running condition); the shop sold her a new ignition module. *20/20's* hidden camera caught the mechanic installing the new module, noticing that the car still wasn't fixed, then discovering the unplugged injector. After plugging it back in, the car ran fine, but the shop charged the reporter for the new module, even though it clearly wasn't needed.

In Arizona, *20/20* said the first 3 Goodyear shops they visited did a good job fixing their staged problem (a blown fuse for the air conditioner), but a fourth shop said the struts were leaking and needed to be replaced. *20/20's* experts said the struts were in perfect shape.

Out of 18 visits to Goodyear shops in several states, *20/20* said they were sold unnecessary repairs 22% of the time (4 out of 18 visits).

After hearing that the TV show was being done, Goodyear made a public announcement that it was ending sales commissions for its mechanics. *20/20* interviewed several current and former Goodyear mechanics on camera, who talked about the pressure to sell unnecessary repairs just to meet their quotas. One mechanic said that they would "oversell as much as possible just to make each manager's quota and keep our productivity up."

When asked what happened after the company ended commissions, one mechanic said the pressure was off for a couple of weeks, "then it went right back to the same old thing—selling as much as we can to keep our productivity up." (One of my "spies" told me that Goodyear's repair shop sales dropped severely the month after commissions were ended.) Another mechanic said he was told that he had to sell $500 per day, $2500 per week; if he didn't do that in three weeks, he'd lose his job. He was fired three weeks later.

In the broadcast, Goodyear said mechanics caught selling unnecessary repairs *may* face disciplinary action, but mechanics said they may lose their job if they don't meet sales quotas. (In most chain stores, there's far more evidence of the second threat being carried out than the first.)

After it aired, Goodyear said the *20/20* broadcast was an example of slanted and deceptive journalism.

**1993-94.** In November '93, Channel 5 (WMAQ-TV) in Chicago, Illinois started an undercover investigation similar to the one done in 1992 by Channel 2 (KSTP-TV) in Minnesota. The undercover cars were put in "top-running condition" by a master mechanic, then they were triple-checked by a AAA consultant for the Chicago Motor Club and a diagnostic company. Once again, the targets were Goodyear company-owned stores.

Reporters for Unit 5 took the cars to company-owned Goodyear Auto Centers in Chicago, asking for full inspections at 13 different stores. At 6 of the stores, Unit 5 said mechanics recommended a variety of services, including tune-ups (with new caps and wires), brake jobs (with new rotors), transmission services, shocks, tires, struts, and cooling system flushes. Reporters authorized some of the recommended services and received bills for $485...$297...$652...for repairs on cars already in top-running condition, cars that even the other 7 Goodyear stores claimed did not need any work.

Four mechanics from one of the offending stores (and a mechanic who was recently fired) went on record with their explanations: "Get all the money. They're not worried about the customer." (John)..."I've been told to do service that doesn't need it." (Dave)..."People are getting ripped-off." (Ken)..."Anything that might make them more money...Fair or unfair." (Jeff)

Unit 5 had copies of Goodyear's sales incentive programs, which explained why some mechanics may have been selling unnecessary repairs. Company memos were found with the following headings: "Special Report," "War Update," and "Alert, Alert." Stores were grouped together for competition, and prizes were offered for the most sales. Those with the highest sales were called "top guns," followed by "hand grenades." "Squirt guns" came in last.

Company officials said that the auto repair industry is based on commissions and those were no more than routine sales incentives. They also said the company has safeguards to protect the consumer, including a whistle-blower hot-line, training programs, and requiring employees to sign agreements promising not to sell unnecessary repairs. Goodyear said they do not tolerate the sale of unnecessary repairs and promised to investigate the allegations, even though they disputed them.

No doubt fearing further erosion in consumer confidence (and company revenue) from the press coverage of the recent investigations, Goodyear announced the end of its sales commission program for mechanics on June 1, 1994. (See Chapter 18, "Are Chain Stores Cleaning Up Their Act?" for more details.)

**1992-93.** KSTP-TV (Channel 2) received a tip that Goodyear Auto Centers were using deceptive sales practices, so the station started a three-month investigation in October of 1992. Using specially prepared undercover cars and hidden cameras, they visited 7 company-owned Goodyear Auto Centers in the Saint Paul (Minnesota) area.

Before sending them to the shops, the cars received new brakes and tune-ups, then they were triple-checked by a diagnostic center, a dealership, and a mechanic/ service advisor to make sure no repairs were needed. Reporters then drove the cars to the shops for their advertised $16 oil change and free brake inspection.

According to Channel 2 reporters, many unnecessary

repairs were recommended; some of the recommended repairs were done, including brake jobs with new rotors (even though the car's brakes were in perfect condition). One shop said the rotors were too thin and needed to be replaced, so after giving permission to replace them, the reporters took the rotors to another Goodyear store to have them checked. The second store measured them and said they were fine.

One car visited the same store twice, but with different license plates the second time. On the first visit, reporters said store personnel told them that the shocks and struts were OK, but the clutch was bad. On the second visit, reporters were told the clutch was OK, but the car needed new shocks and struts.

Channel 2 reporters said that during another visit to one of the stores for the $16 oil and filter special, their car was given a tune-up, even though they hadn't authorized it. When the mechanic noticed that the car already had new spark plugs, and told the manager, reporters said he was told to tune it anyway.

The results of the investigation were aired on TV, using the title, "Taken for a Ride." When they were interviewed, Goodyear company officials said they didn't know those things were going on; they also said they would investigate and take action if they found a problem.

It turned out that the store personnel were on a sales incentive (commission) program, and when company officials were asked if they would discontinue it because of the current problems, they said they didn't know. They also said that (sales commission for mechanics) was the common pay practice for the industry.

As a result of the Channel 2 show, the state attorney general started its own investigation of Goodyear company stores. Current and former store employees were interviewed regarding company sales practices, and a settlement was reached in December of 1993. Goodyear agreed to discontinue its product-specific and service-specific incentive programs (sales contests), pay for arbitration in disputes about the sale of unnecessary or unauthorized repairs, establish safeguards, and contribute $40,000 for consumer education.

## PARNELLI JONES/DOB'S TIRE SERVICE
### Undercover Investigation

**1994.** Parnelli Jones/Dob's Tire agreed to pay $800,000 to settle charges of selling unnecessary parts and repairs. The charges were brought by the California State Attorney General, the Alameda County District Attorney, and the Bureau of Automotive Repair after a two-year investigation that was prompted by complaints from 35 customers.

Fifty undercover runs were made targeting 22 of the company's California stores, and investigators said there were overcharges on 90% of the visits. In some cases, agents said they were charged for work that wasn't done. The average overcharge was $218, but some were much larger. On one visit, an agent was charged $427 for semi-metallic brake pads, front and rear shock absorbers, and brake calipers that weren't needed.

To attract customers, the company had been advertising a number of low-priced repairs and services in newspapers. Low-priced repairs and services were also offered in coupon books that were sold to customers, promising hundreds of dollars in discounts.

Formerly known as Dob's Tires, Parnelli Jones Express Tire Service has 90 employee-owned stores in California, New Mexico, Nevada, Missouri, Kansas, and Texas. Only the company's California stores were targeted in the investigation.

## WINSTON TIRE COMPANY
### Undercover Investigations

**1992-93.** After conducting a lengthy undercover investigation of 37 Winston Tire stores throughout the state, the California Bureau of Automotive Repair charged the company with selling unnecessary repairs and billing for parts that were not installed. The Bureau said that in 74% of the undercover runs, the stores tried to sell unnecessary parts and repairs, or bill for parts that weren't installed. According to one of the deputy district attorneys working on the case, overcharges on the undercover cars averaged $189 for shocks, springs, and brake parts.

When the Sears investigation made headlines in 1992, Winston management voluntarily made changes in its sales practices to ensure that the none of their stores were selling unnecessary repairs. (Both companies had been using sales commissions, contests, and other sales incentives.) However, it was too late—they were already under investigation.

To settle the charges, Winston agreed to pay $1.4 million, which included penalties, costs of investigation, and $450,000 in restitution to consumers. The state said Winston cooperated fully, without fighting the charges, and even went beyond the requirements of the settlement in putting safeguards into place to make sure no more problems occur. (See Chapter 19 for details of the new safeguards.)

**1988.** Winston Tire had previously been charged with selling unnecessary repairs in Ventura County (CA) after a 1988 undercover investigation that involved shocks and front end parts. Winston agreed to pay $100,000 in civil penalties, costs, and restitution to settle the charges.

# BIG O TIRES
## Undercover Investigations

**1992-93.** The owners of an 18-store chain of Big O Tire shops in Orange County, California were charged by the Bureau with fraudulent business practices following an undercover investigation into 5 of their stores. (Charges were only made against CSB Partnership, the owners of the 18 stores, not against the parent company or any other franchisees.)

After receiving a number of consumer complaints for the five stores, undercover cars were sent to the shops, where they detected a pattern of selling unnecessary repairs including brake hardware, rear coil springs, shocks, master cylinders, and disc brake calipers. The average oversell was $397.

To settle the charges of fraudulent or misleading statements and advertising, and exceeding repair estimates without authorization, the owners agreed to pay $169,000 in penalties, costs of investigation, and restitution.

**1993-94.** As a result of other unrelated undercover investigations in 1993-94, three Big O Tire franchises in Northern California were also charged with the sale of unnecessary repairs.

# GOODYEAR AUTO CENTERS,
# FIRESTONE SERVICE CENTER,
# BELLE TIRE CENTER
## Undercover Investigation, Michigan

**1989.** Channel 2 TV (WJBK) was planning a show for consumers on auto repair and they wanted to film some repair shops trying to sell unnecessary repairs, so they asked the Michigan Bureau of Auto Regulation which shops they should visit. They were told to go to the ones that advertised heavily in the local newspapers for low-priced alignments and brake jobs, or free inspections.

The station had a two-year-old vehicle thoroughly checked by automotive experts at the Bureau and at the engineering firm of ECS/Roush, who verified that the front end and brake systems did not need any repairs. Male and female reporters were fitted with hidden microphones, then they took the car on a "shopping" trip to twelve repair centers in the Detroit area for an alignment or brake inspection.

It's interesting to note here that the target shops were chosen solely on the basis of their ads for low-priced repairs and/or free inspections. They were not chosen based on consumer complaints.

Channel 2 reporters said that four of the shops misrepresented the need for repairs by telling the reporters that the vehicle needed new struts or brakes. Two of the shops were Goodyear Auto Centers (one of which was company-owned), one was a Firestone Service Center, and the other was a Belle Tire Center.

According to Channel 2, employees at both Goodyear stores told the reporters that the car needed new struts (MacPherson strut cartridges). At one of the stores, the reporter was told, "You got one strut here that's beating the snubber on the ground, too. It's been coming down and beating the snubber right out of it. Boom! Boom! You getting any noise out of it?" However, the camera showed that the snubbers were still in excellent condition; you could even read the GM logos and part numbers that were on them. Reporters claimed the Goodyear store also said the tires needed to be replaced, but the Bureau expert who checked the tires said he saw no reason to replace them.

At the Belle Tire store, the reporter was told the alignment couldn't be done because the struts were bad. The following conversation was recorded with the hidden microphone: (mechanic) "We recommend that, since they're going bad now, not to align it." (reporter) "You didn't align it?" (mechanic) "No—it won't hold an alignment." (What makes this statement outrageous is that even if the struts were bad, it still wouldn't be true.)

A Channel 2 reporter went back to the shops (with a camera and microphone) and confronted them with the allegation that they had tried to sell repairs that weren't needed, but the shops defended their diagnosis. The tapes were aired in the station's five-part series on auto repair, which included a message from the Bureau on how consumers can avoid rip-offs.

In defense of their diagnosis, one of the shops allegedly claimed that Oldsmobile recommends strut replacement at 45,000 miles. (The car used was an Olds with 43,000 miles.) A General Motors spokesman called the station to say that wasn't true—GM has no mileage replacement recommendation on struts. The company said shocks should only be replaced when they're worn out.

In 1974, Channel 2 did a similar investigation of 25 repair shops which indicated that 1/3 of the shops were dishonest, and 1/3 were incompetent. That investigation was instrumental in getting the state legislature to pass a tough auto repair law.

# 4

# Tune-up Shops

Have you ever wondered why tune-ups are often advertised for $29 to $39 at those "quick tune" shops, when
dealership service departments and independent repair
shops charge $80 to $120? Did you think the tune-up
shops were cheaper because they were tune-up "specialists," so they could get the job done faster and pass the
savings on to their customers? Or did you think the other
shops were just a bunch of evil, greedy capitalists? Well,
like the cheap muffler and brake ads, there's often a catch
to these advertised "bargains."

First, getting a low-priced tune-up is like getting an
oil change without a new oil filter—you might think your
car was serviced, but the job was only half-done. And

second, there's often a hidden agenda behind those low-priced ads: They're designed to attract new customers so the shops can sell them a lot of additional repairs. *They just didn't want you to know.*

### What You Get In a Cheap Tune-up

What do you get in a cheap tune-up? If you have a four-cylinder car, you get four spark plugs—period. That's it. Sure, their ads sound like they're going to do a lot of important stuff, but read the fine print: no more parts, just spark plugs. Here's an actual ad from a major tune-up chain.

> "TUNE-UP SPECIAL, 6 CYL. $39.98, Includes: Complete engine analysis; Check fuel & emission systems; Measure exhaust emissions; Install new spark plugs; Inspect filters, belts & PCV; Check & set timing, carburetor & idle speed; 8,000 mile/8 month guarantee, whichever comes first; Standard ignition & Additional parts extra."

They used 45 words in their ad to make their service look impressive, but if you read it closely, you'll see that the only parts they install are the spark plugs. This isn't even a basic, maintenance tune-up that would be recommended in your owner's manual every 30,000 miles. (On most cars, the spark plugs and the fuel filter should be replaced every 30,000 miles, so that's the best time to get a tune-up. And if it hasn't been that long, you probably don't need one.)

Notice the last line in that tune-up ad: "Additional parts extra." What parts? Some you really need, and some you may not. But either way, you'll pay extra, sometimes a lot extra. Just the fuel filter alone could cost anywhere from $20 to $50 plus labor, changing their cheap tune-up into one costing at least $60 to $90.

About those "checks" and "inspections" that their ads say they're going to do: don't count on it. Several investigations have found that many of these shops don't always check or inspect the items mentioned in their ads.

### What You Get in a Real Tune-up

What do you get in a "real" tune-up? By that, I mean a tune-up done by a dealership or independent repair shop that costs $80 to $120. Their tune-ups typically include the installation of new spark plugs, fuel filter, PCV valve, rotor (if equipped), and an air filter if it's needed. They'll do all of the checks and adjustments mentioned in the ad, too. Since they're getting paid more money for the tune-up, they have time to do a more thorough job. And they usually have a lot more training and experience than the typical "quick tune" mechanic, so they can do a better job of diagnosing problems.

### Advertising for Low-Priced Services

Like the major tire and department store auto centers, these shops are constantly advertising many low-priced services. From newspaper and radio ads to those pesky junk-mail fliers and coupons, they're always having some kind of "special." Oil changes are offered for $12 to $16, tune-ups for $29 to $39, and some advertise brake jobs for $49 to $59.

At those prices, if the shops don't find something else to sell, they won't make any money (and neither will their employees). So why do they run those cheap ads? To bring in a lot of new customers so they can sell them additional repairs. *And because they have no choice.*

One would think that with all those new customers in addition to their existing (repeat) customers, they would have too much business. But they don't. And that's one of their little secrets: Many of these shops have burned so many customers through incompetence or fraud that they could never survive on repeat customers alone. If they stopped advertising those cheap repairs, many of them would quickly go out of business.

Several investigations have documented incompetent repairs and services at many of these shops, and I have witnessed many of them myself. In two recent investigations of Econo Lube N' Tune shops, dozens of consumer complaints were made against their shops. When KNXV did their investigation of several Econo Lube shops in Phoenix, the station found that there were 9 Econo Lube shops in the area with unsatisfactory records at the Better Business Bureau. (And that's pretty hard to do. No wonder they don't have enough repeat business.)

## Incompetence, Faulty Repairs

Incompetence is a major problem in a lot of these shops. Since practically all of their customers are there because of low-priced ads, the shops can't take in enough money (honestly, that is) to hire top-notch technicians. So most of their mechanics are low-paid, poorly trained, fairly inexperienced workers known as "parts changers." They may not be any good at diagnosing problems, but they are often real good at changing (and selling) parts.

Among automotive professionals, a real tune-up expert is known as a "driveability technician." This isn't someone who just knows how to screw in spark plugs; it's a person who can properly diagnose and repair all types of carburetor problems, electronic ignition, fuel injection, computerized engine controls, and emissions systems.

Less than 5% of all mechanics would qualify for this label, and they are usually the highest paid in the business. In major cities, it's not uncommon for these guys to be making $20 to $25 per hour, and they usually have no trouble finding jobs.

## Deceptive Advertising

A lot of the ads run by these shops are dishonest, false or misleading, deceptive advertisements. And here's why: First, they're almost always run with the intention of selling additional parts and services to as many people as possible, but their ads promote ridiculously low prices for services with notes saying, "most cars." When they're caught selling unnecessary repairs in undercover investigations, the standard excuse is "those parts need replacing because of mileage."

By claiming that cars needed fuel filters, PCV valves and other items because they were thought to have been in the cars for over 30,000 miles—even though the parts were brand new—they've exposed their dirty, little scheme. They're admitting that cars with 30,000 miles (or more) need a lot more than just spark plugs, proving my point that their ads are deceptive. Since most cars with less mileage than that don't even need tune-ups, and the shops plan to sell additional parts on cars that are over that mileage figure, their low-priced, "most cars" ads are deceptive.

Because of their heavily advertised, low-priced specials, few of these shops could afford to hire good mechanics on a salary or hourly wage basis, so they usually pay them a low salary plus a commission on the sale of additional parts and services. Obviously, this type of compensation is hazardous to consumers because it often leads to the sale of unnecessary repairs. And that's deceptive business practice #2: failing to disclose that their workers are on commission, when that information would certainly be important to consumers in evaluating any recommendations from those shops.

Deceptive business practice #3: running ads to convince the public that they are a low-priced shop, when a lot of the additional (unadvertised) parts are cheap, low-quality parts that are installed—and billed—at premium prices. In many cases, customers could get better parts (that would perform better and last longer) at other shops for the same prices, or less.

Those practices are bad enough, but some of these shops have figured out how to make a 100% profit on the parts and services they sell: through "phantom sales."

## Phantom Sales & Other Scams

"Phantom sales" is the practice of charging for parts and services that are not actually delivered. On low-priced services, if the workers aren't going to do additional repairs, they might skip parts of the service that people won't notice—like not checking all the fluid levels on a "lube and oil," or not checking the timing, idle speed, and ignition system on a cheap tune-up. If they're caught, they can just apologize and make it look like an honest mistake. *But shops running this scam are rarely caught.*

Many of these shops also recommend fuel injection service to practically every customer, claiming that it's recommended every 25-30,000 miles as "regular maintenance." That's totally unnecessary—injectors should only be cleaned when a vehicle has a driveability problem caused by dirty injectors.

In fact, on many late-model cars, frequent cleaning of injectors can damage them, resulting in repair bills of $500 to $1,000 to install new ones. (This is another good reason to avoid shops with low-skilled workers—they can damage your car.) Also, most vehicles built since 1990 have "deposit-resistant" injectors that make cleaning a waste of time—and money.

In some shops, practically every customer who comes in for a low-priced oil change or tune-up is told that they need a new PCV valve, fuel filter, injection cleaning and/ or transmission/differential service (even though those items weren't checked first). Customers who come in for low-priced brake jobs are often sold calipers, wheel cylinders, rotors, drums or other high-priced parts that aren't needed. And, in fact, many large tune-up chains have been caught doing just that.

## TUNEUP MASTERS,
## ECONO LUBE N' TUNE,
## PURRFECT AUTO SERVICE
### Undercover Investigation

**1998.** Seven Tuneup Masters, 6 Purrfect Auto Service, and 4 Econo Lube N' Tune shops were all caught recommending unnecessary repairs in a huge undercover investigation that was done by KCBS-TV. The shops were all located in Southern California. (Dozens of other chain stores were also caught in this sting. See Chapter 1 for more details.)

Examples of attempted rip-offs, according to KCBS: A Tuneup Masters shop tried to sell them a fuel system cleaning, fuel filter, coolant flush, tune-up and transmission service (total: $278). And a Purrfect Auto shop tried to sell them a transmission service, differential service, fuel filter, PCV valve, oxygen sensor and fuel injection cleaning (total: $363). The station's experts said none of those repairs were needed.

(As of 6/98, a total of 41 Econo Lube and 15 Purrfect Auto shops have been charged with fraudulent business practices in the state of California alone.)

## ECONO LUBE N' TUNE
### Undercover Investigations

**1996.** After receiving a number of consumer complaints against local Econo Lube shops, KNXV-TV ("News 15") conducted an undercover investigation in the Phoenix area. The station used a AAA approved repair shop (recommended by the local Better Business Bureau) to prepare their undercover vehicle, giving it a complete checkup. Their Ford Explorer got new spark plugs, wires, filters, PCV valve, and a radiator flush with new coolant. The transmission and differential were first checked, then seals were put on the plugs to see if the shops checked the fluids.

The vehicle was double-checked to make sure that it did not need any additional services, other than an oil change, then a female producer took it to three local Econo Lube shops. At the shops, she asked for their lube and oil special. She also asked them to "look it over, too—see if anything needs to be done." And they did.

The first shop recommended a new fuel filter and injection service for $75. The second shop recommended a new fuel filter, injection service, new PCV valve, and an oxygen sensor for $197. The third shop recommended a new fuel filter, injection service, new PCV valve, a tune-up, and servicing of the radiator, differential, and transmission for a total cost of $273. Recommended services at the three Econo Lube shops totaled $545, all unnecessary according to News 15 and their expert. News 15 also said the shops failed to check their fluid levels.

**1996.** Three Econo Lube shops in Carson City, Reno,

and Sparks were sued by the Nevada State Attorney General's office after an undercover investigation was done. The shops were accused of cheating customers by not delivering the safety inspection they had advertised as part of their lube and oil change special. Undercover cars were used, and the attorney general said the shops consistently failed to check various fluid levels that were part of the safety check. The shops paid fines to settle the suits.

**1995.** Econo Lube N' Tune Inc. agreed to pay a settlement of $284,776 over charges of fraudulent business practices at its company-owned shops in California. After receiving dozens of complaints about the shops, the Bureau of Automotive Repair conducted a two-year undercover investigation that documented a pattern of overselling at the shops. The company was charged with selling unnecessary repairs, and also with charging for parts that were not installed.

At the time of the investigation, Econo Lube had 18 company-owned shops in California, and operated a total of 210 shops (mostly franchises) in 10 states.

**1994.** Six Econo Lube shops (five in Southern California and one near Sacramento) were busted by the Bureau of Automotive Repair. Four of the shop owners had their licenses permanently revoked, and one received a 90-day suspension.

**1990.** Five Econo Lube shops in Sacramento, California were charged with performing repairs that were not needed and charging for repairs that were not done. All five shops were franchises owned by the same person.

The state attorney general represented the Bureau in an administrative action to suspend or revoke the repair licenses of the franchises. The Bureau had received dozens of complaints against the five shops, and an undercover investigation of them had previously been done.

According to Deputy Attorney General Roy Liebman,

undercover vehicles in perfect working order were taken to the shops by BAR agents, who were charged $200 to $300 for repairs in spite of the vehicles' condition. Liebman said the agents requested the $18 oil changes and $39 tune-ups that were advertised, and they were sold various kits, filters, and other parts, none of which were necessary—the shops replaced gas filters that had only been in the car for seven miles, and performed transmission work when overhauls had recently been done.

Liebman also claimed that BAR agents were charged for repairs that were not done. He said the Bureau had put a covert seal on the differential which was still intact after the shop charged the agent for servicing it.

The owner of the franchises was confronted with the evidence, and he entered into negotiations to settle the charges. Then the Bureau discovered that his shops were still selling unnecessary repairs, so it filed an action to suspend or revoke the shops' repair licenses.

Shortly after the investigation was publicized, the parent company terminated the franchise agreements for the five shops.

Those shops are still in business, but they are now under new ownership. Legal action was still pending against the previous owner, who left the state and was later found working in another chain of "fast-and-cheap" lube, tune and brake shops in Nevada.

## QUALITY TUNE-UP SHOPS
### Undercover Investigation

This investigation is an old one, but it was included for two reasons: 1) because most of these tactics are still being used by other low-priced tune-up shops, and 2) it's a good illustration of how few consumers realize that they were sold unnecessary repairs. Out of the 70,000 people eligible for restitution, only about 125 filed complaints.

**1984.** The California Bureau of Automotive Repair had received numerous consumer complaints regarding questionable business practices at Quality Tune-Up shops, so an undercover investigation was conducted.

When the investigation was completed, a consumer protection lawsuit was filed by the state based on over 100 complaints, 14 undercover runs and information from 8 former employees of the tune-up chain. Out of 40 shops belonging to the chain, 28 were named as defendants.

The tune-up shops were charged with selling spark plug wire sets and electronic ignition sets that weren't needed, using scare tactics to sell unnecessary parts, failing to perform repairs in a competent manner, and operating bait and switch schemes.

Quality Tune-Up had been advertising tune-ups for $39.95 to $49.95. According to the deputy attorney general, there was a consistent pattern of customers being told that the tune-up could not be done because the vehicle had faulty ignition (spark plug) wires. He said these customers were then sold electronic ignition sets and wires that added $25 to $100 to the basic tune-up price.

New ignition wires (that were treated to look old) were installed on undercover vehicles that were then taken to the shops for tune-ups. Investigators were told that their vehicles needed new wires, when the wires actually had about six miles on them.

To settle the charges, the shops agreed to pay civil penalties and investigative costs totaling $430,000—plus restitution for up to 70,000 affected customers. (Total restitution: at least $1.5 million.) This was the largest automotive repair settlement in the state (at that time).

# 5

# Muffler Shops

Why should you have a regular repair shop replace your muffler for $120 when you can take it to someone who's advertising the same repair for only $29.95? Especially when the cheaper shop says that they're the only ones with a "lifetime" muffler? Because there's often a catch to those advertised bargains: People rarely get out of the "low-priced" shop without spending a lot more money, and those lifetime guarantees are usually worthless—or worse yet, another scam.

As mentioned in the first chapter, "bait and switch" ads are a form of deceptive advertising, a dishonest, illegal business practice. In the muffler business, this involves advertising a muffler (or other exhaust service) for a low price with the intention of selling more expensive repairs to most of the people who go to the shop for the advertised item.

Some of the common tricks that are used on customers are: telling them that the advertised muffler will not work well on that particular car (or that it won't last that long), claiming that additional parts are needed before they can install the muffler (like clamps, hangers, and exhaust pipes), and trying to "upsell" the customer to a premium muffler with a lifetime guarantee.

## The "Rusted-Out" Excuse

If a shop says they can't install a new muffler without first replacing the exhaust pipes—because they're "rusted out"—be sure to check them yourself (or get a second opinion) before authorizing the additional repair. Even though this can be a legitimate excuse, it is often used dishonestly to sell expensive repairs.

How can you tell if a part is too rusted or not? A light coating of rust on the surface of exhaust pipes, mufflers, or converters is perfectly normal and will not prevent a good welded installation. A part doesn't need to be replaced if it doesn't leak, or if it only has light surface rust.

However, if a part is so rusted that its surface has bubbles or scales on it, or if the part can be punctured with a screwdriver (using normal hand pressure), then it probably needs replacing. In some parts of the country (by the ocean or where roads are salted in the winter), exhaust parts may rust quickly. In other areas, those same parts could easily last 100,000 miles or more.

## Catalytic Converters

Using the "rusted out" lie, dishonest shops will try to convince customers that their catalytic converters need replacing. (They love doing converters, because they usually generate a $300 to $400 repair bill for installing just one part.) *Don't fall for this!* Converters often last for at least 100,000 miles (or as long as the car), and if they fail within 7 years or 70,000 miles, they're probably covered by the manufacturer's emissions warranty that applies to all owners of a vehicle, not just the original owners.

If a shop says your converter is bad, ask them to show you the proof, then get a second or third opinion—and another estimate—before you allow them to replace it. (I know this is inconvenient, but so is paying $400 for a converter that you don't need.)

## Lifetime Guarantees

"Lifetime guarantees" on mufflers are almost always a scam. First, the price on a lifetime muffler is going to be higher than that of a regular muffler. Second, most of the shops offering these wonderful guarantees have no intention of actually replacing them for free without requiring customers to pay for additional high-priced repairs. (Don't forget: These shops are in business to make money, not to do free repairs.)

Finally, if your original muffler lasted 80-90,000 miles, the rest of the vehicle might be ready for a trade-in (or the junkyard) long before the replacement muffler goes out again.

## MIDAS MUFFLER & BRAKE SHOPS
### Undercover Investigations

**1994.** Midas was forced to change its advertising practices in early 1994 after an investigation by the New York State Attorney General's office. The company had been advertising new mufflers for $24.95 (with a disclaimer that additional parts are often needed at substantial extra cost), and the investigation found that only 5% of their customers got a muffler for the advertised price.

In fact, 95% of consumers who went to Midas for the $24.95 muffler paid, on average, over four times the advertised price. (A 1989 investigation of Meineke Mufflers came up with similar results.) The attorney general said that Midas ran the ads to lure consumers into their shops, where they were sold expensive additional repairs. (How else did you expect them to pay for all those ads?)

**1989.** To settle state civil charges of deceptive advertising and selling unnecessary repairs, nine Midas Muffler & Brake Shops agreed to pay a judgment of $400,000 and Midas International (the parent company) agreed to pay another $100,000. The charges resulted from a three-year investigation by the California Bureau of Automotive Repair and four district attorneys' offices who had targeted the Midas shops after receiving numerous consumer complaints. The shops were all individually owned franchises and were located in four counties.

One of the deputy district attorneys who worked on the case claimed that the muffler they had advertised for $18.95 did not exist. He said that an additional $6 charge for clamps, hangers, pipes, or welding was added to all $18.95 muffler jobs.

Advertisements for automotive service are required by law to disclose the likelihood of additional charges. The type used for this disclosure must be at least one-half the size of the type used for the advertised price.

The muffler ads used by those shops did offer some disclosure, but the wording and the type size did not comply with the law. The parent company quickly changed its advertising when it was contacted by the district attorney's office.

A permanent injunction was entered against all Midas Muffler & Brake Shops in California prohibiting the sale of unnecessary parts and repairs, and advertising to install mufflers unless the advertised price includes all charges. (This settlement also involved brake and suspension repairs from a 1986 investigation. See Chapter 2, "Brake Bandits," for more information.)

## ADDITIONAL ADVICE

If your vehicle is in a muffler shop for exhaust work, hopefully you have already checked the shop out using the methods mentioned in this book so you are sure that they can be trusted. If not, the best way to avoid being sold unnecessary parts and repairs is to wait at the shop while they do the work, and to insist that they show you what parts need to be replaced so you can make an informed decision.

Beware of muffler shops that pressure you to replace the catalytic converter. Muffler shops don't usually have the equipment or the training to diagnose a converter as the cause of higher emissions, and if your vehicle actually ran that bad because the converter had failed, you probably wouldn't be taking it to a muffler shop to get it checked out.

Also, watch out for shops that try to charge you for adapters they claim are necessary to install a new muffler. When they mention adapters, you'll know they're not installing the right muffler, but instead are trying to install one that's cheap and in-stock. All mufflers are not the same, and if the wrong one is installed, driveability and/ or emissions problems may develop.

Before you give the OK for new exhaust pipes or other repairs, check the parts yourself using the guidelines in this chapter. If they don't look bad to you, but the mechanic claims they are, don't get into an argument with him. Just say that you can't have any more work done at that time and they will have to put your vehicle back together so you can drive it home. (Then you can take it to another shop for a second opinion.)

A difficult situation can arise if you are told that they can't put your vehicle back together unless they install the new parts that they've been trying to sell you. Details on what you can do if you find yourself in this predicament are given in Chapter 13, "Avoiding Rip-Offs."

Instead of going to different shops to get work done at the lowest prices, going to the trouble of taking your vehicle to another shop to get a second opinion, or wondering whether the additional repairs you bought were really needed, try to find a mechanic you can trust using the guidelines in this book. You will probably end up saving money in the long run because you won't be paying for a lot of unnecessary repairs.

If you have found a reputable repair shop with well-trained mechanics, but they don't do muffler work, ask them to recommend a good muffler shop. Most mechanics know which shops in their area can be trusted to do an honest, high-quality job.

# 6

# Department Store
# Auto Centers

Many of the large department stores have automotive service departments that benefit from the name recognition and large advertising budgets of their parent companies. The biggest ones are found at Sears and Montgomery Ward; Macy's, Emporium, and Weinstock's also have auto centers at some of their stores. Kmart's auto centers were recently sold to racing legend Roger Penske; they're now called "Penske Auto Centers."

Like the large tire and auto centers, these stores were designed to offer high-quality service at low prices, and their mechanics were supposed to be well-trained in the repairs and services that were offered. Customers were led to believe that these centers were run with the highest levels of honesty and professionalism. While many people have received honest, competent service from some of these shops, many others have been victimized by faulty repairs or the sale of unnecessary parts and services.

Again, like the large tire and auto centers, some of the department store auto centers have a long history of selling unnecessary repairs. After running ads for low-priced tires and alignments, they would then try to sell a lot of ball joints, idler arms, shocks, and other suspension parts that weren't always needed. People who came in for low-priced brake jobs, cheap oil changes, or free inspections were often sold drums, rotors, calipers, wheel cylinders, master cylinders, and other unnecessary parts. Because this was being done by well-known companies, most people never suspected they were being ripped off. It came real close to being the perfect scam—except some of them got too greedy, and they were caught.

### Deceptive Advertising

False (or deceptive) advertising has been commonly used by many large auto centers, especially in the area of brake services. Low-priced brake ads that say "Brake Reline (most cars)" or "Brake Service (most cars)" are almost always deceptive.

The average brake job at most large auto centers costs between $160 and $200, so the companies know that "most cars" are not going to get a brake job for $59 or $69. At the very least, the semi-metallic brake pads that most cars require will cost an extra $20 to $25. (And that's before they try to sell you new calipers, wheel cylinders, rotors, drums, etc.)

### Their Secret Practices

What most people didn't know was that practically all of the major auto repair companies (including department store auto centers) had been using some form of sales quotas, commissions, and/or contests to encourage the sale of additional repairs. A large part of employees' pay was often based on sales, with poor sales figures resulting in reprimands, demotions, or even termination. Sears got caught running contests that rewarded the auto center employees with the highest sales, and Kmart was doing the same thing for its management personnel.

## Quotas

Most (if not all) of the major auto centers have some type of monthly sales quota for their store managers, with pay linked to total sales and/or profits. Companies usually deny having "quotas," but admit to having "sales goals" with major consequences attached (like termination). *Those are really quotas.* Many also have "goals" for their service (sales) associates, who are usually paid a sales commission on repairs and services that they recommend to customers.

In the past, mechanics in department store auto centers all received some type of salary plus commission on sales, but most of that has ended. Instead of sales commissions, most of the large auto centers now use "productivity goals" to motivate their mechanics. (They're really quotas.) This practice is supposed to sound better (for consumers) than commissions, but is it really?

The use of productivity goals for mechanics would be OK if all the repairs and services they performed were based on realistic prices. However, since a lot of the work these mechanics get is based on advertised low-price specials, they either have to rush through every job—which would explain the faulty repairs done by some of these stores—or they have to find other (higher-priced) repairs to sell.

The bottom line is: when mechanics feel pressured to

meet their quotas, or they're just trying real hard to earn a living under impossible circumstances, customers will be sold unnecessary repairs.

## Low-Priced Advertising vs. Quotas

At these stores, the goal has consistently been to try for higher gross monthly sales, and with all the low-priced ads they run for repairs and services, about the only way to accomplish that is to sell a lot of higher-priced parts. (After all, they are "mass merchandisers." Their goal is to sell as much merchandise as possible.)

Had consumers known about the sales practices of the major companies, they probably wouldn't have trusted any recommendations that were given. And if customers knew about the deceptive advertising that was used to get them into the stores, so they could be sold more expensive repairs, they would have trusted those companies even less. *And that's why they didn't want you to know.*

## KMART AUTO CENTERS
### Class-Action Lawsuit

**1994.** A class-action lawsuit was filed against Kmart over allegations of fraud in its auto centers. The company was accused of using an incentive/quota system that encouraged the sale of unnecessary repairs, using false and misleading advertising, making false and misleading statements and material omissions to its customers.

Even though the lawsuit was certified as a class action in federal court, it has bounced around from court to court as Kmart fights to get rid of it. It was thrown out again, on a technicality, and the plaintiff's lawyers refiled it in another state. (Documents from the lawsuit are mentioned in Chapter 1.)

As mentioned earlier, all of the Kmart Auto Centers were sold to Roger Penske, who renamed them "Penske Auto Centers." His company announced that they would keep all of the existing employees.

## SEARS AUTO CENTERS
Undercover Investigations—
California, New Jersey, New York, Florida

**1992.** On June 11, the California Department of Consumer Affairs announced that the state Bureau of Automotive Repair was seeking to revoke the repair licenses of all 72 Sears Auto Centers in the state, charging them with false or misleading statements, fraud, false advertising, and willful departure from accepted trade standards. The Consumer Affairs director stated, "These are not honest mistakes. This is the systematic looting of the public."

The charges against Sears were the result of a 15-month undercover investigation by the Bureau of Automotive Repair which started in December of 1990. After detecting a pattern of consumer complaints against Sears, the Bureau conducted 38 initial undercover runs at 27 of its repair shops, documenting the sale of unnecessary parts and services 90% of the time. The average bill for unnecessary repairs was $228; in some cases agents were charged as much as $550 for repairs that weren't needed.

The Bureau also claimed that in some cases, Sears employees used scare tactics to sell repairs, telling agents that certain brake parts were defective and unsafe, when they were in perfect working order. Agents said that Sears' mechanics made incompetent repairs—some cars were damaged, and one undercover car that went in for a brake inspection left the shop with no brakes.

After the initial investigation, Sears was notified of the results by the Bureau. The following month, undercover agents made 10 more visits to Sears' shops and documented the sale of unnecessary repairs 80% of the time. According to the Bureau, the number of items oversold was lower on the second round of visits.

Sears initial response to the charges was an angry denial of any wrongdoing, claiming that "the Bureau's undercover investigation was very seriously flawed..." and that the company would fight the charges in court. However, three days later, the New Jersey Division of Consumer Affairs announced that it had been conducting an (unrelated) undercover investigation of Sears Auto Centers and had documented the sale of unnecessary repairs during 12 visits to 6 Sears shops. Then the Florida Attorney General's office notified Sears that its repair shops were being investigated.

Due to the bad publicity, sales at Sears Auto Centers dropped 15-20%. Since its auto centers contributed about 9% of Sears' total revenue, the sales drop could have cost Sears $400 to $500 million over the course of a year. On June 22, the chairman of Sears admitted that "mistakes did occur" at shops in California and New Jersey, and promised to eliminate commissions and sales goals at the shops.

How did Sears get into so much trouble? They had been advertising free brake inspections and brake jobs for $48 to $58 to bring in customers, and their service advisors were on a commission/quota system that encouraged the sale of unnecessary repairs (especially the five items listed below). Employees who failed to meet their quotas were often disciplined by having their hours cut or being transferred to another department.

In September, a settlement was announced by Sears and the California Department of Consumer Affairs. Sears agreed to pay $8 million to settle the charges: $3 million for restitution, $3.5 million for costs of the investigation, and $1.5 million worth of tools and equipment for the state's community college system. Sears was allowed to continue operating repair shops in the state, but they faced suspension if their shops violated the terms of the settlement during the next three years.

To settle the charges of selling unnecessary repairs in California and New Jersey, Sears agreed to offer restitution to any consumer nationwide who purchased a pair of brake calipers, a pair of coil springs, a pair of shock absorbers, a master cylinder, or an idler arm from August 1, 1990 to January 31, 1992. The company said that more than 900,000 consumers may be eligible. For those consumers who weren't satisfied with the coupon offer, Sears said it would honor its policy of "satisfaction guaranteed or your money back."

An investigation into Sears' auto repair practices by the New York Attorney General's office revealed more embarrassing problems than those uncovered in California, including the widespread employment of service advisors with little or no previous training or experience in auto repair. In spite of their obvious lack of qualifications, their job description included inspecting and diagnosing vehicles prior to making service and repair recommendations to consumers.

At the Sears centers, the principal function of the service advisors was to generate sales of auto repair services and products. Their pay was based on an incentive compensation plan consisting of a minimal base salary plus commission that was tied directly to their total sales, so the more they sold, the more they were paid. In addition, the company ran contests to see who could produce the biggest increase in sales for specific parts or services.

The New York Attorney General claimed that unnecessary repairs were sold at Sears as a direct result of their "incentive compensation and goal-setting program," and that Sears service advisors often refused to honor lifetime service contracts they had sold for wheel alignments and other services, unless vehicle owners agreed to pay for additional repairs.

According to the New York State Attorney General, the practices found at Sears were being used nationwide, and by other companies as well. Following the investigations, Sears discontinued most of its sales incentive programs and put into place a number of safeguards to protect consumers.

## MONTGOMERY WARD AUTO CENTERS
### Undercover Investigations

**1998.** Six Montgomery Ward Auto Express stores were caught recommending unnecessary repairs in a huge undercover investigation that was done by KCBS-TV in Southern California. One example: According to KCBS, an Auto Express store tried to sell their investigators front and rear brakes, wheel balancing and alignment (total: $429), when none of those repairs were needed. (Dozens of other chain stores were also caught in this sting. See Chapter 1 for more details.)

**1995.** Montgomery Ward agreed to pay $765,000 to settle fraud charges against three of its Auto Express stores in California (two in San Jose and one in Sacramento). An undercover investigation conducted by the Bureau of Automotive Repair confirmed the sale of unnecessary repairs, charging for repairs that were not done, and incompetent repairs at the Auto Express stores.

After receiving consumer complaints against the two shops in San Jose, the Bureau made six undercover visits to those shops. According to the Bureau, agents were sold unnecessary brake repairs, and they were charged for alignments that weren't done, on 5 out of 6 visits. (The only alignment done by the shops was done improperly.) Two of the agents were sold higher-priced "four-wheel" alignments on cars with non-adjustable rear wheels (i.e., rear wheel alignment was not possible).

As part of the settlement, the company agreed to distribute coupons worth almost $300,000 to customers who paid for alignments and brake repairs, and refunds totaling $14,816 for the 26 customers who filed complaints. The individual refund checks ranged from $23 to $2,300.

**1988.** Montgomery Ward paid $112,500 to settle charges of performing illegal smog inspections at its Riverside (California) auto center. The charges resulted from an undercover investigation by the Bureau of Automotive Repair.

**1983-85.** Over a three-year period, district attorneys in two different counties filed separate consumer protection lawsuits against Montgomery Ward, Inc. for alleged unlawful and fraudulent business practices at its auto centers. The state Bureau of Automotive Repair had received numerous consumer complaints against the auto centers, so they conducted undercover investigations.

The first investigation was in Stanislaus County. When the investigation was completed, the district attorney filed suit against Montgomery Ward, claiming that its auto center was using unlawful business practices. They were accused of recommending unnecessary repairs, performing unnecessary or unworkmanlike repairs, misrepresenting the condition of parts on customers' vehicles, and damaging or sabotaging parts on customers' vehicles so that further repairs were required.

To settle the charges, Montgomery Ward paid fines and costs totaling $80,000 and agreed to an injunction prohibiting all company employees in the state from any unlawful business practices.

About two years after the Stanislaus County case, another investigation of a Montgomery Ward Auto Center was done, this time in El Dorado County. The district attorney sued the parent company, claiming that it had used unlawful and fraudulent business practices.

In the lawsuit, Montgomery Ward was accused of the following: charging customers more than the estimated price, recommending unnecessary repairs, making untrue and misleading statements to customers regarding repairs and services, and defrauding customers by recommending and charging for parts that did not need replacing.

The auto center was also accused of charging customers for repairs that had not been done. Some of the unnecessary repairs that they were accused of selling included tune-ups, alternators, voltage regulators, and master cylinders.

To settle the charges, Montgomery Ward paid fines and costs totaling $110,000 and made restitution to 118 customers. The company also agreed to another injunction prohibiting all of its employees in the state from any unlawful business practices, including the allegations listed in the lawsuit.

This Montgomery Ward store was located in a small town (Placerville) and there was a lot of publicity surrounding the case after the district attorney filed the lawsuit. Shortly after the case was settled and the restitution was completed, the store closed.

# 7

# Dealership Service Departments

Back in the "good old days" (for car dealers), new-car sales were so profitable that many dealers looked at their service departments as existing just to service new cars and perform warranty work. Customers who bought cars from a dealer were usually treated better in the service department than those who didn't, since the dealer was really only interested in selling more cars. If he occasionally made some money from paying service customers, that was just icing on the cake, but there was little interest in expanding the service department.

Manufacturers estimate that only 30% of car buyers return to dealers for service after their warranty runs out.

What is it that has driven customers away? Poor service, high prices, and callous service people are often given as reasons for people taking their cars to other shops. And some thought they were sold unnecessary repairs.

Well, there may be good news for consumers who would like to go back to the dealer for service—if they could be sure they would receive better treatment. The good news (for paying customers) is that dealers now care about winning their service business *because they need the money.* People have been keeping their cars longer, and there are too many dealers selling the same cars, so competition has kept prices (and profits) down. Service and parts made up about 50% of the average dealer's profit in 1993, so they can't afford to turn their backs on paying service customers anymore.

Although there are still dealers out there who would rather have your money than a good reputation, it looks like many have been moving in the right direction. In the 1994 *Consumer Reports* survey, dealership service departments came in second in overall customer satisfaction, after independent repair shops. Major chain stores scored much lower, due to more sales pressure, repeat problems, and jobs not completed when promised.

Of course, there are always exceptions, but if a particular dealer has a bad reputation for service, that will usually be common knowledge in the local community. Also, the local Better Business Bureau can provide a rating (by phone) as to how the dealer resolves complaints filed against his business.

## Pros & Cons of Service Departments

Posted hourly labor rates at dealership service departments are usually higher than those at independent repair shops for several reasons. First, dealers have higher overhead because their mechanics are often paid more (and have more benefits) than mechanics working in other repair shops, and dealerships usually have a lot more expensive equipment that is required to work on newer models.

Second, training classes for dealership mechanics are almost always held during working hours (which means they're not working on cars), while mechanics in independent shops usually attend classes at night or on weekends (to reduce the costs to employers).

Overall dealer service prices are also higher because their service departments are not usually willing to give away any labor on a job that turns out to be more difficult than originally estimated. Since each department's profitability in a dealership is constantly monitored by upper management (and accountants), service personnel will usually do whatever it takes to make a profit on every job.

On the other hand, many independent shops will absorb the additional time that is required to finish a difficult job. Sometimes they will even give away parts to avoid creating an unpleasant customer relations problem. When things go wrong, most small shops would rather lose a little money on a job than lose a good customer.

The advantages of using a dealership service department that sells your type of vehicle include: expert knowledge of your vehicle (at least in theory), factory technical information and assistance, factory-trained mechanics (again, in theory), the use of original-equipment parts, and the availability of binding arbitration.

Binding arbitration (through Autocap) is usually available to resolve disputes between dealerships and consumers. There is usually no charge to consumers for this service, and it can save the time and expense of going to court. Decisions are binding on the dealership, but not on the consumer, who is free to take his case to court if he is not satisfied.

Dealership mechanics are *usually* specialists in one repair area of one brand of vehicles (for example, one mechanic might repair transmissions only, while another mechanic might only repair computer systems). Because they have access to factory training and technical assistance that is not usually available to mechanics working in independent shops, dealership mechanics are *usually* more knowledgeable concerning the types of vehicles they work on.

As stated earlier, one of the reasons that dealerships have higher overhead is that their mechanics are usually paid more than those working in other repair shops. Generally speaking, dealership mechanics are paid more because they have had more training and are more skilled in their particular area. (They have to be pretty sharp to repair new cars.)

While it is true that consumers are more likely to find highly skilled technicians (for a particular vehicle) at a dealership, it's not true that *all* mechanics working in dealerships are highly skilled. There is a serious shortage of top-notch mechanics and dealerships are affected, too. I've known quite a few dealership mechanics who were highly skilled, but I've also seen some who were not.

In the past, I've had to repair many vehicles that were either misdiagnosed or improperly repaired by dealership mechanics. In some cases, their mechanics had replaced six or eight computer parts on a vehicle before the problem was fixed. (Although it's sometimes necessary to replace two or three parts to repair a computer system, the only time six or eight parts would need replacement would be if the engine caught on fire or was submerged in a flood. Instead of testing, they were guessing.)

Even though a dealer's posted labor rate may be higher than the labor rate at other repair shops, a dealer can still perform some types of repairs for less money. This is especially true of repairs on computer systems and other high-tech items on late-model vehicles. A factory-trained specialist should be able to diagnose and repair difficult problems faster than a mechanic who works on several (or many) different types of vehicles.

Sometimes a mechanic has to make an educated guess concerning which part to replace. This is where a dealership mechanic has a distinct advantage over an independent—he can usually borrow a new part from the parts department to see if that will cure the problem, and if it doesn't, he can usually return it so the customer won't have to pay for it.

Independent shops can't borrow parts. Once a part is installed, they have to keep it, which means that the customer will have to pay for it even if it didn't cure the problem. This can sometimes result in consumers paying more for repairs at an independent shop than they would have paid at a dealership.

If a particular problem is common to one model, the manufacturer may repair it for free, even though the official written warranty has expired. (This is known as a "secret warranty.") For example, I have seen Toyota dealerships replace some exhaust manifolds on vehicles with 100,000 miles on them, at no charge to the customer. These types of repairs are not widely known outside of dealerships, so customers may end up paying for repairs at independent shops that could have been done for free.

Even though dealerships have factory training and other advantages, they still have trouble finding and keeping good mechanics just like any other business. (One local dealership couldn't perform any smog inspections for a while because it didn't have any mechanics who could pass the new state test for a smog license.) Sometimes new mechanics just don't work out, and a bad one can mess up a lot of cars before he is fired.

The disadvantages of using a dealership service department (that sells your type of vehicle) include: repair bills that are often higher than independent shops for the same repair, not being able to talk to the person who is going to work on your vehicle, and sometimes encountering an indifferent attitude concerning the cost of repairs and whether they will be completed on time.

## Posted Labor Rates vs. "Real" Labor Rates

One of the things to watch out for at dealership service departments is when their "real" labor rate is higher than their posted labor rate (based on actual time spent on the job). For example, an independent repair shop that has a posted labor rate of $50 per hour may charge $75 labor for a front brake job, because the job takes 1.5 hours. However, a dealership with a posted labor rate of $50 per hour may charge 2 hours labor ($100) for the same job, making their actual labor rate $66 per hour, because the repair only takes 1.5 hours.

This is a fairly common practice, resulting in so many complaints that dealerships in some states are now required to post a notice explaining that their labor charges are based on "established times" for particular repairs and may be higher than the posted labor rates for the actual time spent working on a vehicle.

When this method of pricing is used, consumers are not able to make accurate price comparisons based on the posted labor rates. If you call a dealership (or any other shop) to compare prices, make sure you get the total labor charges for a particular repair, as well as a breakdown of the parts to be changed (and their prices) so you can tell what the actual labor rates are.

**Charging for Warranty Work**

Another thing to watch out for at service departments is the practice of charging for diagnosis and/or repairs that should be covered under the warranty. One way this is done is when consumers bring their vehicles in for repairs without knowing that they are covered under the warranty, and the service personnel fail to mention it, so the vehicle owners end up paying for the repairs.

The other way this is done is when consumers expect the repairs to be done under the warranty, but they are given a phony story explaining why the repairs aren't covered or why they'll have to pay for diagnosis. (If a dealership tries to pull this scam on you, ask to speak to the service manager, and if he doesn't resolve the problem to your satisfaction, call the manufacturer's customer service number for assistance.)

Why would a dealership try to charge customers for repairs that could be done under warranty? Two possible reasons: 1) Because the dealer can file a warranty claim anyway and get paid twice for the same repair, and 2) dealers make more money per hour on cash customers than they do on warranty work.

The car manufacturers set limits on how much time they will pay for each repair done under warranty, effectively lowering the amount received by the dealer for every hour worked. For example, a manufacturer may only pay for one-half hour of diagnostic time (even if it takes an hour) for a particular problem under warranty, but a dealership could charge a cash customer one hour or more to diagnose the same problem.

As you can see, dealerships have a major financial incentive to charge customers for repairs that could be done under warranty, so it's wise to question or challenge them if they try to charge you for something that you think

should be done for free. If all else fails, call the manufacturer's customer service number for assistance before paying for diagnosis or repairs.

## Charging for Unnecessary Maintenance

Another outrageous practice at some service departments
involves charging for scheduled maintenance that the
manufacturers say does not need to be done for another
15,000 to 30,000 miles or more. This often involves replacement of parts that could easily last 10,000 to 15,000
miles or more, and in many cases the parts could be replaced for free (under warranty) if they really were defective.

To illustrate how this scam works, we'll use a typical
15,000 mile service. On many cars, the service recommended by the manufacturer might only be a routine oil
and oil filter change, and maybe a tire rotation. A dealer
who wants to "increase his cash flow" would also replace
the spark plugs, distributor cap and rotor, ignition wires,
filters, coolant, and/or transmission fluid. He might even
align the front end. So, instead of paying $30 to $40 for
the factory-recommended service, the customer might
pay as much as $300 to $400—for repairs that are largely
unnecessary.

According to an article titled, "Made-up Maintenance" that appeared in the September 14, 1992 issue of
*U.S. News & World Report*, the above practice seems to
be fairly common. The magazine's investigation included
a survey that was done to find out what services dealers
perform during "scheduled maintenance" visits.

*U.S. News* surveyed 122 dealers in seven major cities
across the country, gathering estimates for service on six
popular late-model cars. Almost 80% of the dealers surveyed added services to the manufacturer's list; 60% also

included replacement of parts that the manufacturer said did not need replacing.

In the article, several dealers tried to defend the additional services, offering excuses of "hot summers, cold winters, humidity, stop-and-go driving," etc. Officials from two automakers disagreed. Mazda's manager of quality assurance was quoted as saying, "Every town has traffic, and most areas have periods of stop-and-go...we don't build cars that are going to have problems because of commuting or air temperature or salt on the roads a few times a year."

According to the *U.S. News* article, Ford's parts and service engineering manager said that dealers may, on occasion, have reason to exceed the manufacturer's maintenance schedule. He gave an example of plugged fuel filters caused by poor local fuel quality that could result in driveability problems, a case that would justify more frequent replacement of fuel filters. (In his example, affected vehicles would exhibit symptoms indicating that a problem exists *before* a vehicle is brought in for routine service.)

The Ford manager also said that manufacturer's "severe service" schedules were designed to include traffic, dust, extreme weather and other harsh conditions, so it's usually a waste of money to let a dealer talk you into additional services.

Two other practices to watch out for were also mentioned in the *U.S. News* article: inflated labor times and "ghost services." The first involves charging several more hours of labor for easy-to-perform services like rotating the tires; changing the brake fluid; adding (usually worthless) additives to the oil, fuel, and cooling systems; and performing quick visual inspections of the suspension and drivetrain.

"Ghost services" refer to the outrageous practice of

charging for work done on items that can't be serviced, don't need to be serviced, or don't even exist. In the *U.S. News* survey, 29% of the Mazda dealers included a valve adjustment in their 15,000 mile service and 38% included it at 30,000 miles. However, according to the manufacturer, all Mazda cars produced in the last five years have self-adjusting valves, including the model used in the survey. (That means the valves can't be adjusted.) Some other popular ghost services: "cleaning/adjusting the choke" on fuel-injected cars (they have no choke), and "adjusting the idle speed" on computer-controlled cars (their idle speed is controlled by the computer).

Aside from the "minor" issues of fairness, honesty and general ethics in business, the practice of "made-up maintenance" can actually be against the law if customers are told that parts are bad when they're not. Shops that recommend unnecessary repairs can find themselves in serious trouble. The following stories of two dealerships that were accused of doing just that illustrate some of the practices consumers should guard against.

### Undercover Investigation, 1989-90
### Lodi Honda, California

After receiving a consumer complaint against a Honda car dealership in Lodi, California, the Bureau of Automotive Repair and the San Joaquin County district attorney's office conducted an undercover investigation. When the investigation was completed, the district attorney's office filed a consumer protection lawsuit against Lodi Honda, an independently-owned new car dealership, asking for civil penalties of $1 million.

Lodi Honda was accused of charging over 2,000 customers for service that was either unnecessary or never done. According to the Bureau, undercover agents took several Hondas to the dealership, requesting that 30,000 mile services be performed. The Bureau's report claimed that Lodi Honda personnel performed service that was not recommended by Honda Motor Corp. until 45,000 and 60,000 miles. The report also claimed that those services were not explained to investigators until after they had been done. Bureau officials said that they inspected a vehicle after the service appointment and found that some services listed as being completed were not done.

The Bureau's report concluded: "This constitutes fraud, false and misleading statements, and false and misleading documents. It is apparent that Lodi Honda is engaging in unethical and unfair business practices, in that they are charging for services and receiving higher profits at the expense of the consumer."

The owner of Lodi Honda agreed to pay a total of $170,000 to settle the charges. ($20,000 for civil penalties, $35,000 for investigative and legal costs, $115,000 for restitution)

## Undercover Investigation, 1989-90
## Gene Gabbard Honda, California

In a similar case, the owner of Gene Gabbard Honda in Stockton was sued by the District Attorney's office in 1990 over the alleged sale of unnecessary parts while performing 15,000; 30,000; and 45,000 mile services. The Bureau of Automotive Repair said the undercover vehicles they sent in for service already had new spark plugs, distributor rotors and fuel filters, but they were replaced anyway.

The alleged overcharges varied from $40 to $60 for approximately 400 customers. To settle the charges, the dealership agreed to pay a total of $61,000 which included more than $21,000 in restitution.

## How to Protect Yourself

To guard against these practices, consumers should check their owners' manuals to verify that the recommended services are actually required to keep up the warranty. If they are not, refuse the repairs and get a second opinion.

Most tune-up parts, including spark plugs, distributor rotor and cap, and ignition wires are covered under the emission warranty for the first 3 years/50,000 miles, or whenever the manufacturer recommends the first scheduled replacement. (For more information on parts covered under emission warranties, see the "Smog Inspections" chapter.)

## Note on Scheduled Maintenance

Vehicle owners do not have to take their cars to a dealer for scheduled maintenance. It is against the law for a manufacturer or dealer to require that, unless they're going to do the repairs for free.

All that's needed to keep your warranty in effect is to have all the scheduled maintenance done, on time, by a licensed repair facility. Be sure to keep good records, in case the manufacturer or dealer tries to get out of a warranty repair by claiming that your car wasn't properly maintained. And yes, you can change your own oil without voiding your warranty. Just keep the receipts for the oil and filters, and make sure it's done properly.

# 8

# Transmission Shops

John, a typical vehicle owner, doesn't even think about his transmission until he notices that it's no longer working properly. Then, filled with fear that repairs are going to cost hundreds of dollars, he does what he has been conditioned to do by advertising—he takes his vehicle to a "big-name" transmission shop. Why? Because he's been sold the idea that they're experts who can be trusted.

At the shop, John is greeted by several friendly people who promise to check out his car for about $30. He's told that they need to do a fancy inspection and road test, check some things out on the car, then they'll call him with an estimate. But it doesn't sound too bad.

When John gets "the phone call," he's told that it looks like his transmission has some internal problems: "They dropped the pan and found a lot of metal particles inside." Without taking the transmission apart, they say there's no way to tell what's wrong, so they need his permission to do a "tear-down inspection" for about $300. John is told that the $300 includes reassembling his transmission, so he's thinking it might only cost $400 to $500 for the whole thing.

When the next phone call comes, John is hit with real

bad news: "Your transmission's got a lot of problems inside—we found bad gears and drums, broken bands, worn out clutch packs and other stuff—it's gonna take a lot to fix it right. You're looking at $2,500 for everything. Yeah, it's really messed up inside."

John goes into shock—his vehicle was running when he brought it to the shop, and now he's being told that the transmission needs an expensive overhaul. He briefly wonders if all that is really necessary. Then, realizing that his car is completely disassembled in their shop, John authorizes the overhaul. He tells himself, *"A really big company like that wouldn't lie to people. They wouldn't rip me off."*

Did his transmission really need a complete overhaul, or was he ripped off? Well, John will never know for sure, but some of the biggest names in the transmission business have victimized thousands of people by selling unnecessary repairs. And many of them got away with it, because people couldn't believe that those companies would commit such outrageous acts of fraud on so many customers, for so much money. *But they did.*

## Ads for Free Inspections & Low-Priced Services

Like a lot of shops that do brakes, mufflers, tune-ups, etc., transmission shops also do a lot of advertising to bring in new customers. Some of them spend 5-10 times as much on advertising as many other shops, which again brings up the issue of repeat customers and referrals. A shop that has to spend that much money just to stay in business must have burned a lot of previous customers. And who pays for all that advertising? Why, the new customers, of course—usually through huge repair bills that often include overcharging, "phantom sales," unnecessary repairs and other scams.

## Deceptive Advertising

Most of the large transmission companies have already gotten in trouble for deceptive advertising. Some of their old tricks have been picked up by many smaller shops (and some smaller chains) who have been running a lot of deceptive ads over the last few years.

"Bait and switch" is an old scam, and several variations are still in use today. The first involves an advertised low-price service (or free inspection). In this scam, the shop will try to sell major repairs to everyone who comes in for a routine service, whether their cars need work or not. Numerous lies and tricks are used to sell unnecessary major repairs to unsuspecting customers.

The second bait-and-switch scam is the low-priced ad for a transmission overhaul at an "irresistible" price, usually around $199 to $249. (I've seen them as low as $99.) If the shop is really going to do the work, they'll usually call the customer after the transmission is apart to tell them it's going to cost more than they thought. ("We found a lot of bad parts inside; we had no idea it was this bad when we quoted you a price.")

Some shops that advertise cheap overhauls don't even do the work—they just charge people, anyway. After doing minimal repairs on a transmission, they just paint the outside to make it look like an overhaul was done.

## The "Particles in the Pan" Scam

This particular scam is one of the oldest ones in the repair business, but it still works because it sounds legitimate. First, the shop has to get your car inside to take off the transmission pan. (That's why they ran that ad for a cheap service.) Once the pan is off, they show you the thin layer of metal particles in the bottom of the pan, saying that it indicates a major internal problem requiring immediate attention. And that's the lie—a thin layer of metal particles in the bottom of the pan is perfectly normal, even on fairly new cars.

As long as the layer isn't real thick, and there are no large chunks or pieces of internal transmission parts, that is not an indication of a serious problem. And don't put it past some of these guys to plant the material and pieces in your pan. *Keep an eye on them.*

To avoid these types of scams, remember this: If your transmission worked fine on the way to the shop, there's probably nothing wrong with it. Don't be fooled by scare tactics like this: "If you don't get it fixed right now, you could experience total transmission failure, with no warning, leaving you stranded somewhere."

### "We Have No Idea How Much It Will Cost"

If you hear anything like this from a transmission shop, you'll know they're dishonest (or very stupid): "We have no idea how much it could cost, without taking it apart first. That's why we need your permission for a tear-down inspection."

Without disassembling a transmission, any honest transmission shop can give an exact price for a "soft-parts overhaul," which includes all labor to remove, rebuild, and replace the transmission, along with internal clutches, bands, gaskets, seals and fluid. The only parts that should be additional are "hard parts"—gears, shafts, drums, etc. (parts that don't normally wear out).

It is necessary to disassemble a transmission to check the hard parts, though, so the initial estimate might be increased later. But an honest shop will tell you the range of possible repair costs. Also, exchange transmissions are almost always available at a fixed price, so if your transmission needs too many hard parts, an honest shop will recommend installing an exchange unit instead of fixing yours. (Ask if this is available before they start.)

**The Tear-Down Inspection**

Tear-down inspections are a legitimate part of the transmission business that has been misused by dishonest shops to trap customers into paying for expensive repairs. As mentioned in previous sections, tear-downs are necessary to inspect the hard parts inside a transmission, but an honest shop will disclose the total labor charge and the range of possible total costs before they take someone's car apart.

**Lifetime Guarantee Scams**

Like the "lifetime guarantees" that are used in brake and muffler shops, these guarantees are often used to trick customers into paying outrageous prices for transmission overhauls and paying for repairs that aren't necessary. These are almost always a bad price—and a bad deal.

# AAMCO TRANSMISSIONS
**Undercover Investigations**
(California, Iowa, Louisiana, Massachusetts, Michigan, Missouri, New Jersey, New York, North Carolina, Ohio, Pennsylvania, Tennessee, Texas, Utah, Washington, West Virginia, Wisconsin)

**Background.** Because Aamco has such a long history of investigations, charges and allegations involving fraudulent business practices, older information is mentioned first, leading up to newer information at the end. The following information is by no means all-inclusive; it's just the most significant items that were readily available.

**1970.** After investigating the practices of Aamco Transmissions, the Federal Trade Commission obtained a consent order barring the company from using deceptive practices in the repair and rebuilding of automotive transmissions. In the order, Aamco was prohibited from misrepresenting products or services to obtain leads for major transmission repairs, furnishing others (franchisees) with deceptive advertising material, and promising "one-day service" when it is not available.

**1981.** Following a three-year investigation by the Bureau of Automotive Repair, a civil suit was filed by the State of California against Aamco Transmissions, Inc. and 18 of its franchisees. In the suit, Aamco was charged with deceptive advertising because its ads for "free multi-check" and "free road test" did not disclose that a teardown inspection (for which there would be a substantial charge) was necessary to diagnose internal transmission problems.

The individual shops were charged with the following: recommending or selling unnecessary repairs; misrepresenting the condition of customers' transmissions; representing or implying that parts or services have been provided when they have not; representing or implying that metal particles in a transmission pan indicate a major transmission problem when it is not true and without telling customers that metal particles appear in every transmission pan, even on new vehicles.

Aamco and the shops agreed to a settlement that included payment of $100,000 in civil penalties and investigation costs by nine of the franchisees, in addition to court orders prohibiting Aamco and the franchisees from the unfair practices listed below. (Nine other Aamco franchisees named in the original suit had gone out of business during the settlement negotiations.)

**1987.** A settlement was reached that ended a two-year investigation of Aamco Transmission Centers by the attorneys general of 14 states. (California, New Jersey and Utah were not part of this group.) As part of the settlement, Aamco agreed to pay $500,000 to the states for investigation costs.

Aamco also agreed to consent orders which prohibit the company and its franchisees from the following: using bait-and-switch tactics or other deceptive sales practices; misrepresenting that a tear-down inspection or other major repairs are required; misrepresenting that repairs have been made; collecting for repairs that have not been made; collecting for repairs which said defendants know or reasonably ought to know are unnecessary; refusing to provide estimates before transmissions are disassembled; altering parts of customers' motor vehicles with the intent to create a condition requiring repairs.

The consent decree also ordered the parent company to set up a program to monitor customer complaints, and to take specific action against franchises that receive too many complaints during a six month period. Aamco investigators were to conduct undercover "shopping" runs at franchises receiving three or more complaints in one category. Franchises that failed a "full-scale shopping" by recommending and providing unnecessary major internal repairs were to be sold or terminated.

Before the consent decree, Aamco shops would not give estimates to customers until after their transmissions were disassembled, a practice that is now prohibited. Because of this, and the publicity surrounding the investigation and settlement, many Aamco franchisees have reportedly suffered substantial drops in revenue, some as much as 50%.

It appears that the investigation also caused a significant drop in the number of Aamco shops in the country. Some of the states involved in the investigation claimed that many of the Aamco shops in their state went out of business shortly after the settlement was publicized. In February of 1987, a company spokeswoman stated that the company had 900 locations. In November of 1990, the number given by the company was "about 700."

What started this multi-state effort? Numerous complaints were filed against Aamco with the consumer protection agencies in the 14 states. According to one of the attorneys general who worked on the case, investigators found 2500 instances of customer complaints that they were charged for repairs that weren't requested, weren't needed, or weren't even done.

Investigators claimed that many of the complaints concerned Aamco's refusal to honor warranties and repair charges that they called "unconscionable." (Some people were charged as much as $2300 for a transmission overhaul on a GM vehicle that only would have cost $700 to $800 at most other shops.)

Almost all of the states involved used undercover investigations to build their cases. Agents were fitted with hidden microphones to record statements made by the shops to sell repairs. The cars that were used had either completely rebuilt transmissions or ones that were in perfect working order, except for minor external problems that were created immediately before the car was taken to a shop.

The problems that were created were usually a disconnected vacuum hose at the modulator or misadjusted linkage, both of which would cause shifting problems. Shop manuals and accepted trade practices dictate that those items be checked before any internal repairs are attempted. (Only the most inexperienced or incompetent transmission mechanic would not know this.)

In Missouri, undercover agents shopped 5 St. Louis Aamco stores a total of 15 times, using 3 different cars with completely rebuilt transmissions. Sometimes the modulator hose was disconnected before they went to the stores, but other times the transmission was in perfect working order with no symptoms. Complete overhauls were recommended and sold 13 times out of the 15 visits.

In Michigan, the Bureau of Automotive Regulation conducted the undercover investigation. According to the Bureau, undercover cars with rebuilt transmissions and no problems were sent to shops for routine service (fluid change, etc.), where agents were sold complete overhauls for $400 to $900.

The Michigan Bureau claimed that one of the Aamco stores sabotaged the transmission on an undercover car so it would fail. The agent (who was wearing a hidden microphone) brought in a car that had a rebuilt transmission and no problems. After the shop serviced the transmission, he was told that it might start slipping, and that if it did, it would need major repairs. The Bureau said the transmission did start slipping within minutes, because the shop had loosened the band adjustment to make it slip. The shop was charged with sabotage.

In Wisconsin, the investigation started after an Aamco shop manager walked into the office of a Department of Justice investigator. He said his conscience had been bothering him, and he had to tell someone what had been going on at the shop. The shocking story that he revealed was backed up by an ex-mechanic from the shop who testified for the state.

According to the investigator, the Aamco manager documented 95 cases (from the two shops he managed) of customers who were charged for repairs that were unnecessary, or were not even done. The manager said that the shop routinely charged customers for rebuilt torque converters, when the old ones were just cleaned and repainted. (The Justice Department later found four state fleet vehicles that the Aamco shop had supposedly put rebuilt converters in, but had actually just repainted them.)

The Aamco manager told of one instance involving a manual transmission that had been disassembled for an inspection, and nothing was wrong with it. However, the shop owner told the customer that the bearings were bad, and when the customer told him to save the old bearings, the owner instructed the mechanic to ruin the bearings with a torch. The customer was then told that the bearings were so bad that they had to be cut out with a torch. (The shop foreman also testified that this story was true.)

## Aamco Transmissions: After the "Big Bust"

Did the investigation and settlement in 1987 put an end to allegations of unlawful and fraudulent business practices at Aamco shops? While investigators admit that the number of complaints has dropped dramatically, they have not dried up completely. (With 200 fewer Aamco stores now than there were in 1987, and the new requirement to give written estimates before doing a tear-down inspection, the number of complaints should have dropped.)

**1989.** One Aamco shop in Oceanside charged with making false or misleading statements and committing a fraudulent act, following undercover investigation by the California Bureau of Automotive Repair. Settlement included: shop closed for 4 days with sign posted explaining reason for closure, plus 5 years probation.

**1989.** The New Jersey Attorney General's office targeted 3 Aamco shops in an undercover investigation. A civil suit was then filed charging them with selling unnecessary repairs. To settle the charges, the shops paid civil fines and agreed to consent decrees prohibiting them from using unlawful business practices.

**1990.** A class-action lawsuit was filed against Aamco claiming that the company used deceptive advertising to lure purchasers of transmission services into paying more than they should have paid, and to induce them to pay for unnecessary repairs. Aamco settled the case out of court.

**1990.** Five Aamco franchise owners filed suit in federal court against Aamco Transmissions, Inc., claiming that senior Aamco officers have threatened and harassed shop owners to prevent them from exposing a company scheme to defraud customers.

Aamco claimed that the five were trying to ruin the company's reputation and encourage other shop owners to renege on their franchise agreements. Some franchisees had taken sides with the five who filed the lawsuit, while others had sided with the parent company.

The five Connecticut shop owners accused Aamco of encouraging some franchisees to perform unnecessary repairs to increase revenues. In the lawsuit, they made the following accusations.

> "The basic and constant scheme is to lure customers into Aamco franchises...cause them to believe they have a major internal transmission problem, then get them to authorize removal and disassembly of the transmission....Finally, when the transmission is disassembled and [customers] are at a bargaining disadvantage, [the Aamco representative offers] them only the choice of either a fully rebuilt transmission at prices significantly above the competitive market price, or having no work done and having the transmission reassembled for a substantial price."

In the lawsuit, they accused Aamco of allowing some franchise owners to stay in business despite a history of fraud. (If this is true, it would be a violation of the consent orders that Aamco signed in 1987.) The documents identified 58 franchisees who allegedly used unlawful and/or fraudulent business practices.

Despite investigations by state and federal authorities, the five claimed in the lawsuit that the alleged scheme to defraud consumers has continued.

The franchisees later dropped their lawsuit against the parent company. When asked about the claims made by his clients in the suit, their attorney said, "The parties have amicably resolved their differences and don't believe any purpose would be served by any further comment."

## COTTMAN TRANSMISSIONS
### Undercover Investigations

**1990.** Cottman Transmission Systems Inc. agreed to change its business practices and pay $60,000 to settle charges of selling unnecessary repairs brought by the Missouri State Attorney General. The charges were a result of an undercover investigation that was initiated by over 100 complaints against the shops in 3 years.

The investigation documented 5 cases where Cottman shops recommended major overhauls when only minor, if any, repairs were needed. Cottman shops were also refusing to disclose repair costs prior to inspections that involved disassembling transmissions, and there were numerous complaints that the shops failed to honor warranties and charged more money than the agreed-upon estimates. A former employee said that a company manual gave instructions on how to avoid giving customers repair estimates before the car was brought into the shop.

**1989.** Following an undercover investigation, two Cottman Transmission shops were charged with recommending unnecessary repairs by the New Jersey State Attorney General. To settle the charges, the shops paid fines and signed consent decrees.

**1988.** Cottman Transmission Systems Inc. was sued by the Maryland State Attorney General after their investigation found a pattern of fraudulent business practices at 11 out of 13 Cottman shops in that state. The trial judge ruled that Cottman was guilty of deceptive trade practices and ordered it to pay a $100,000 fine. A higher court later ordered the company to make restitution to customers who were sold unnecessary repairs.

Cottman had been training shop managers and employees on how to withhold pricing information from customers until their cars were in the shop and their transmissions were disassembled. Their shops had been telling customers that they had no idea how much a transmission repair would cost without first taking it apart, when the shops did know exactly how much a "soft-parts overhaul" would cost. The attorney general also presented evidence that some Cottman shops had charged for parts that were never installed.

## LEE MYLES TRANSMISSIONS
### Undercover Investigations

**1987.** Three Lee Myles Transmission franchises were the subjects of an undercover investigation by the Arizona State Attorney General's office. The investigation was done in response to numerous consumer complaints that had been filed against the three shops.

The attorney general's office said the shops had run continuous ads for low-priced transmission services (at $4.95 to $9.95) to attract customers, then when the services were being done, they would show customers the metal particles in the pan (that were normal) and say that was evidence of internal problems. They would also tell customers the fluid was burnt and that it indicated internal problems, to get authorization for tear-down inspections.

Investigators said that customers were not given estimates before their transmissions were disassembled. The shops told people that they had no idea how much repairs would cost without disassembling the transmission. Investigators claimed that after a transmission was taken apart, in almost all cases the shops told customers that major repairs were needed.

Undercover cars with completely rebuilt transmissions were sent to the shops and the agents were wired to record what was said. To create a problem requiring repairs, a hole was punched in the rear seal, causing it to leak. (Since the transmissions were already thoroughly rebuilt, the only repair that was needed was a new rear seal. Including parts and labor, that should have cost about $50 to repair.)

The following story of what happened at one of the shops was taken from the investigator's notes and the recording that was made from the undercover wire.

> Warren Poole [the undercover agent] took the car to the Indian School Road shop on June 29, 1987, and told "Chip" [a shop employee] that the transmission was leaking. After an external examination was performed, "Chip" told Poole that various parts of the transmission were leaking (in addition to the rear seal) and that there was metal in the transmission pan which meant that something was breaking up inside. "Chip" told Warren the transmission had a "problem," and that it needed to be taken apart and inspected (for a charge of $150, which would be credited toward the repair cost if the repairs were done at that shop). Poole asked how much the repairs would

cost and "Chip" assured Poole that "It's not gonna be that costly."

After the transmission was taken apart, "Chip" told Poole that a number of parts were damaged and that the total cost of repairs needed was $791.33. The work was done and Poole did in fact pay $791.33 for it.

The tape of this undercover is especially interesting, because "Chip" assured Poole at least twice that "We're here to help you, not to rip you off." "Chip" also disparaged other transmission repair shops, saying that "We're not like some transmission places that are out to rip you off" and that "AAMCO stands for 'All Automatics [transmissions] Must Come Out.'"

The attorney general's office filed a civil suit against the three Lee Myles shops (which were all owned by one person), accusing the shops of the following: deceptive and fraudulent business practices, recommending unnecessary repairs, charging for parts and services that were not provided, and representing themselves as "transmission specialists" and "experts" when their repair work was often of poor quality.

In December of 1988, a judge found the accusations to be true and ordered the defendants to pay $50,000 for restitution, and $2,500 for civil penalties. All owners, officers and employees were prohibited from any ownership or employment connected with repairing or servicing motor vehicles for a period of ten years.

**1989.** Four Lee Myles Transmission shops in New Jersey were charged with fraudulent business practices following an undercover investigation by the state attorney general's office. To settle the charges, the shops paid fines and signed consent decrees.

**Other Undercover Investigations**

Shops from the following chains have also been charged with unlawful and/or fraudulent business practices in the service and repair of transmissions:

California — Gibraltar Transmissions, Mr. Transmission, Interstate Transmission, Trans-King

Florida — Aaction Transmissions, Transmission Express, Transmission World, Speedy Transmissions, Transmission Kingdom

Michigan — A-1 Transmissions, American Transmission, Interstate Transmission, Royal Transmission

New Jersey — Gibraltar Transmissions

Tennessee — Mr. Transmission*

Utah — Mr. Transmission

*Civil suit filed by attorney general based on numerous complaints against 29 shops; no undercover work done. Case settled, consent order issued.

## MANUAL TRANSMISSION GUIDELINES

It's not always necessary to rebuild a transmission to cure shifting problems—the solution could be as simple as a loose shifter bolt or pin. If the transmission will only go into gear when the engine isn't running, it may only need a new clutch master or slave cylinder, or it may need a new clutch. A bad clutch (that isn't releasing completely) can also cause hard shifting or grinding when changing gears.

Hard shifting or lock-up in gear can be caused by a loose or missing shifter bolt, improper shift linkage adjustment, bent shift rod levers, or shift rod lock pins that were incorrectly installed or have fallen out. On many vehicles, these problems can be repaired without removing or rebuilding the transmission.

Beware of shops that say a transmission needs to be rebuilt before they've done an inspection. If internal repairs (or overhaul) are necessary, the transmission must be disassembled before an accurate, final estimate can be given.

If your transmission needs to be rebuilt, and several expensive "hard parts" are needed (for example, gears or shafts that cost over $100 each), it may be a lot cheaper to install an exchange transmission than to repair the one that was in your vehicle. Be sure to ask if this option is available *before* bringing your vehicle in for major repairs.

## AUTOMATIC TRANSMISSION GUIDELINES

If a vehicle is brought in for repair immediately after a problem develops, it's often possible to repair the transmission without an overhaul. This is especially true if it had been properly maintained (i.e., the fluid was changed regularly and never got burnt).

Sometimes an overhaul is necessary to cure what seems like a minor problem, especially if the transmission was low on fluid or slipping for a while before it was brought in for repairs. When the fluid level is too low or slipping occurs, excessive friction and heat are created which can quickly destroy the transmission. Fluid that is discolored or smells burnt may indicate overheating and possible internal damage.

Most fluid leaks can be fixed without removing the transmission from the vehicle. However, it is necessary to remove the transmission to replace the front seal. As long as the transmission was properly maintained and no slippage occurred, it is not usually necessary to overhaul it to repair leaks.

Regular maintenance of an automatic transmission will greatly reduce the likelihood of expensive repairs being needed before the vehicle has at least 100,000 miles on it. Most transmission specialists recommend servicing every 15-30,000 miles, depending on driving conditions. Servicing should include fluid and filter change, band adjustment, and inspection.

If your vehicle needs a transmission service, take it to a transmission shop or a regular repair shop. *Don't take it to one of the "fast and cheap" lube and oil shops.* The workers in lube and oil shops generally have no experience or knowledge of automatic transmissions, so they wouldn't be able to perform any of the inspections or adjustments that should be done when a transmission is serviced.

It may be too late to start servicing a transmission if it hasn't been done for at least 50-60,000 miles. Servicing it at this point could cause leaks to develop, or even complete transmission failure, if the accumulated varnish that is preventing seals from leaking is cleaned out. It may be safer not to service it, and to just drive it until the transmission needs an overhaul.

If you take your vehicle to a transmission shop for routine service or major repairs, and you're not sure that they are completely honest, be sure to wait at the shop while they remove the transmission pan.

The pan must be removed to make an inspection and give an estimate for repairs. Even if you had no problems with the transmission and only brought it in for a routine service, they could find an excessive amount of metal or clutch material in the pan, indicating the need for major repairs. Beware of shops that give repair estimates without removing the pan for inspection, especially if they say your transmission needs to be rebuilt.

There are two important reasons for you to watch while they remove the pan: one, so you can see for yourself if there really is excessive metal or clutch material in the pan; and two, to make sure the pan they are showing you came from your vehicle (and not from someone else's). If you're not watching, an unscrupulous mechanic could put metal in your pan or show you the metal in someone else's pan, and you wouldn't even know it.

A thin film of gray material in the pan is normal. Large (i.e., easily noticeable) metal particles or piles of clutch material usually indicate major problems, even though the transmission may have worked fine before it was brought in. However, heavy deposits in the pan may be normal on some transmissions if the vehicle has a lot of miles on it, so be sure to get a second opinion before agreeing to a major overhaul because of this.

An honest transmission shop won't object to a customer waiting at the shop and watching while the pan is removed for inspection. (Due to insurance regulations, they probably won't allow you to stay inside the shop, but you can usually watch them remove the pan from outside.)

Beware of shops that object to your waiting and watching while they remove the pan. If they start making excuses about why you shouldn't (or can't) wait and watch, you should take your vehicle somewhere else for inspection and repairs.

It's not always possible to give an accurate, final estimate for a transmission overhaul before it is completely disassembled. Most estimates given before disassembly include labor and "soft parts" (gaskets, seals, clutches) only.

When the transmission is disassembled, they may discover that some "hard parts" (gears, drums, converter, etc.) are worn and need to be replaced. One new hard part (for example, a gear) can cost over $100, so a revised estimate can be considerably higher than the original one.

Don't automatically assume that you are being ripped off because they call after taking your transmission apart to tell you that it's going to cost more than they originally thought. An honest, professional shop will always warn customers of this possibility before any work is done, so beware of shops that fail to tell you this up front.

If your transmission is in really bad shape (i.e., it was slipping for a long time or the fluid is badly burnt), it may be a lot cheaper to install an exchange transmission than to repair the one in your vehicle. Be sure to ask if this option is available before bringing your vehicle in for major repairs.

## SUMMARY

When your transmission acts up, don't take it to a transmission shop just because they do a lot of advertising—take the time to locate a reputable repair shop that employs highly skilled technicians, and take it there first. (See Chapter 15, "Finding Mechanics You Can Trust.") If you don't, you may end up paying thousands of dollars for transmission repairs that aren't really needed.

If you have found a great repair shop, but they don't do transmission work, ask them to recommend a good transmission shop. Most mechanics know which shops in their area can be trusted to do an honest, high-quality job.

Make sure you get a detailed, written estimate before anyone works on your vehicle. Without disassembling a transmission, an honest shop can give an accurate estimate for a "soft-parts overhaul," which includes all labor, gaskets, seals and soft parts necessary for an overhaul.

# 9

# Service Stations;
# Robbery on the Interstate

As a general rule, many service stations are only interested in performing repairs that are "quick and easy." Few stations have enough room to do major repairs that could tie up a service stall (or parking space) for several days or weeks, so they usually turn away jobs that they think are difficult or will take a long time to complete. This is especially true in the areas of major engine and transmission repairs, electrical work and computer problems.

Service station mechanics normally have to work on all types of vehicles, from domestics and imports to cars and trucks, which prevents them from becoming extremely knowledgeable concerning any one type. So, although they can usually diagnose and repair the easy problems on many different kinds of vehicles, they are normally unable to handle the hard ones. Many stations regularly refer their customers to dealerships or other shops for jobs that are too difficult for them.

Most service stations' weakest area is their lack of training and skills concerning late-model cars. (This is generally true of all types of shops, not just service stations.) Their strong points are: convenient locations, the acceptance of oil company credit cards for repair bills, and prices that are usually lower than independent repair shops and dealership service departments.

Service stations can sometimes be convenient and inexpensive places to get quality work done on routine auto repairs and maintenance. Some of the repairs they excel in are: lube and oil changes, (maintenance) tune-ups, brakes, cooling systems, air conditioning, minor electrical problems, and front end work.

Make sure you choose a shop that only employs ASE certified technicians who receive continuous training to keep up with the latest technology. If your area has AAA Approved Auto Repair Facilities, choose a shop that is in that program. (See Chapter 15, "Finding Mechanics You Can Trust," for more information.)

## "Superstations"

Some stations do have mechanics who are highly skilled and able to handle difficult problems, but they are definitely in the minority. These stations should be easy to spot—they'll usually have the latest equipment and a booming business, too. Since highly skilled mechanics are hard to find, word travels fast when someone finds a shop that is able to diagnose and repair problems that other shops couldn't fix. I've seen a number of these "superstations" that have sophisticated diagnostic equipment and at least 3-4 highly skilled technicians.

**Service Station Scams**

Consumers have been ripped off in two ways by service stations in the past—from being sold unnecessary repairs due to incompetent diagnosis in some cases and fraud in others. Some stations only rip off an occasional customer, while others make a serious effort to rip off as many as possible. And many service station mechanics are paid a commission on the parts and labor they sell, a practice that encourages the sale of unnecessary repairs.

In an outrageous example of auto repair fraud, some service stations located out of town on lonely stretches of highway have used scare tactics and sabotage to sell unnecessary repairs. While pretending to check the oil or tires, unscrupulous mechanics have cut fan belts, hoses and tires; some have even squirted oil on shock absorbers or other parts so they would appear to be leaking.

After the sabotage is done, the customer is called over to look at the problem that was just "discovered." The hook that is used to trap the victim is the warning that the vehicle is not safe to drive, that it will never make it to the next town. Since most people would not want their car to break down on a deserted highway, it's fairly easy to victimize motorists with this scam.

To prevent this from happening to you, have your vehicle checked thoroughly before any trips, and never leave it unattended when stopping for gas. Keep an eye on attendants who are checking your oil or tires.

**Undercover Investigation—
Service Stations in Arizona**

According to the Arizona Attorney General's office, most of the auto repair fraud in that state occurs at service stations located out of town on the highways. These stations are independently owned and carry the names of most (if not all) of the major oil companies.

Unlucky motorists stopping for self-service gas have been sold unnecessary coil springs, shock absorbers, tires, fan clutches, alternators, and repairs on transmissions and differentials. Coil springs were the most common, because they are a fast, high-profit item, followed by shocks and tires.

The Attorney General's office had received numerous consumer complaints against a particular service station, which was located in a remote area on an interstate highway, so an undercover investigation was done. A female agent was wired to record the conversation, then she drove a motor home to the service station for gas.

A station employee came out and took a look at the tires on the motor home, then informed the agent that the tires should be replaced because they were damaged. (He said they were "coming apart or separating.") When the agent told him that the tires were new (they only had about 1,000 miles on them), he changed his story. He then told her that the tires were the wrong size and load rating for the motor home, and that they weren't safe to drive on. Naturally, the station happened to have the "proper" tires on hand.

At this point, the agent agreed to buy a new set of tires and requested that they put her old tires (the ones that only had 1,000 miles on them) in the back of the motor home. After leaving the station, she checked the tires they had put in the back and discovered that they were someone else's old tires, not the new ones that had been on the motor home.

The agent went back to the station and demanded that they return her tires, and they eventually did. (Apparently, the station had planned on keeping her tires to resell to someone else.)

# 10

# Body Shop Scams:
# The Invisible Fraud

Body shop fraud is believed to be a widespread problem, but few consumers are even aware that they have been ripped off. As long as the external finish of a rebuilt vehicle looks good, most consumers assume that all of the repairs were done properly (even when they're not), so dishonest shops are able to commit "invisible fraud" that can go undetected for years.

According to the insurance commissioner of New Jersey, the cost of body shop fraud to insurance companies in that state is estimated at $240 million a year, resulting in higher premiums for motorists. On a national level, the Society of Collision Repair Specialists put the cost of fraudulent body shop schemes at about $5 billion a year. However, since most of the fraud is hidden from view, even those estimates could be far too low.

Fraudulent body shop practices can involve any (or all) of the following: charging for new parts when old parts were just repaired, using aftermarket parts instead of OEM (original equipment) without permission or disclosure, charging for new parts when used parts were installed, or charging for repairs that were not done as specified on the estimate or invoice.

## Evidence of Fraud

Numerous investigations of body shops in different parts of the country have shown that fraud is easy to find. An undercover agent in New Jersey received 48 bribes from 17 body shops while posing as an insurance appraiser. Undercover police in California made over 70 arrests at body shops and wrecking yards (auto recyclers) that bought parts they thought were stolen. In Florida, agents from the state insurance department ran a sting using a fictitious insurance adjusting firm. They claim that body shop managers offered them bribes to inflate insurance company payments by thousands of dollars.

In a 1993 insurance company investigation, 692 vehicles that needed $2,000 or more in body repairs were reinspected at shops that had been selected by the vehicle owners. The first round of reinspections indicated that fraud had occurred 60% of the time because the shops had changed the method of repair without the knowledge or permission of the insurance company or vehicle owner. The estimates were readjusted downward on the remaining 40% because reinspections indicated that some of the repairs were not necessary.

In 1994 the California Bureau of Automotive Repair analyzed the insurance company's reinspection data from 52 vehicles that had an average repair cost of $5,161. On 40% of the vehicles, some form of fraud was found, plus repairs were so substandard that they caused a devaluation of the vehicles. Only 29% of the vehicles had acceptable repairs that returned them to the same condition they were in prior to the accident.

## Faulty/Incompetent Repairs

Incompetent repairs by body shops appear to be an even larger problem than fraud. According to the Bureau of Automotive Repair's 1994 Auto Body Report, a survey of body shops in Northern California rated 30% of the shops in 16 counties as incompetent in basic auto body repairs, and 80% of the shops in 28 counties as incompetent in major rebuilding of vehicles. Of all the shops responding to a statewide survey, only 11% had a full-time technician certified by ASE for metal work, only 12% had a full-time technician trained by I-CAR, and only 50% had the equipment necessary to properly repair vehicles.

Faulty repairs can cause significant economic losses for vehicle owners. Vehicles that are not properly repaired may be worth only a fraction of their value before an accident, and any unrepaired damage that is not discovered until a later accident will be considered "pre-existing damage" that isn't covered by insurance.

Vehicles that are not properly repaired may also be unsafe in a collision. Most new cars built since the early 1980s have what's known as "unibody" construction, a design that provides more protection for occupants in a collision. Special training and equipment is required to properly repair unibody vehicles and restore their structural integrity.

## Are Insurance Companies Encouraging Fraud and/or Sloppy Repairs?

For most body shops, 80-90% (or more) of the repairs they do are paid for by insurance companies. In an effort to hold down the cost of their claims, insurance companies exert tremendous pressure on shops to keep repair costs down. This is why body shop labor rates are usually about 30% lower than those of general automotive repair shops, even though their labor costs and other overhead are about the same.

Insurance companies have several ways of keeping repair costs down. The two most common are refusing to pay a body shop's posted hourly labor rate and its estimated time to repair a problem. For example, a shop may have a labor rate of $45 per hour, but the insurance company might say that they'll only pay $40 (or less), and when a shop estimates that a repair will take 11 hours the insurance company might decide to only pay for 9 hours (or less).

If shops aren't paid enough to do repairs properly, many will start cutting corners to save money. Top-notch body and paint technicians cost a lot to have on the payroll, but trying to save money here by hiring lower-paid, less-skilled workers almost always results in poor-quality repairs that are quite visible, so shops usually have to find other ways to save (or make) money.

Instead of taking the time to do a conscientious, professional job (that they might not be getting paid for), shops may cut corners by doing repairs as fast as possible, resulting in poor quality repairs that may not be visible on the outside. They can also use other, more "creative" ways to increase profits as a way of compensating for the insurance companies' lower payments. The legal term for this is "insurance fraud," the practice of charging for parts that aren't installed and repairs that aren't done. (This is also common in the medical profession, where it's known as "cost shifting" and Medicare fraud.)

Another trick insurance companies use to reduce costs is telling shops to install less-expensive aftermarket parts instead of original equipment (OEM). This practice is usually a bad deal for everyone except the insurance companies.

## Aftermarket vs. Original Equipment Parts

Insurance companies will often insist on the use of after-market body parts because they are less expensive than original equipment (OEM) parts. However, aftermarket parts are not crash-tested as are OEM parts, they usually don't have the same corrosion protection, and they often don't meet the car manufacturer's specifications for over-all quality, weight, fit, and finish. In addition, OEM parts usually offer much better warranty protection than after-market parts.

Many body shops (and other automotive experts) say that aftermarket parts take longer to install because they don't fit as well and often result in lower-quality repairs that could even reduce a vehicle's resale value. Insist on the use of OEM parts.

## How to Find a Good Body Shop

Wise consumers use the same criteria for choosing a body shop that they use for other types of auto repair: a good reputation, highly skilled technicians, proper equipment, and emphasis on quality repairs. *Don't choose a shop based on its advertising.*

To check on a shop's reputation, ask people in the area what kind of experiences they've had with the shop. Ask your mechanic which body shops do the best work, then call the local Better Business Bureau to see if they have a satisfactory rating. And don't be afraid to ask a shop to show you their credentials; look for diplomas or certificates that verify training in the types of repairs they perform. Visit the shop to see some of the cars they've just repaired and inspect them closely.

To find well-trained technicians, look for shops that employ mechanics trained by I-CAR. If they're also certified by ASE in damage repair and structural analysis, that's also a plus. I-CAR has a toll-free number to help consumers find shops that have used their training; call 800-ICAR-USA for the shop nearest you. (I-CAR stands for the Inter-industry Conference on Auto Collision Repair, a non-profit training organization that specializes in auto body repair. ASE stands for the National Institute for Automotive Service Excellence, another non-profit group that specializes in certification of mechanics.)

### Clipping or Sectioning Vehicles

"Clipping" or "sectioning" refers to the practice of cutting off part of a car (sometimes as much as one-half) and welding on another section from a different car, instead of installing new parts or totalling the vehicle. If this is done without the knowledge and consent of the owner and the insurance company, it would be fraud.

This procedure must be done by a highly skilled technician. If it is not done properly, the result could be a vehicle that is devalued significantly and one that may be unsafe in a collision. Before considering this type of repair, make sure the mechanic has the proper training and certification. (I-CAR offers training for this procedure.)

### Low-Priced Paint Jobs

Beware of low-priced paint jobs. A high-quality, long-lasting paint job requires careful preparation and application by well-trained and highly skilled technicians, so a low-priced "special" is going to have a catch. Shops offering paint specials will have to sell other higher-priced repairs to make money (that's the real reason they spent money advertising a cheap service) or they will have to cut corners to get the jobs done quickly.

Sloppy preparation and application will result in a paint job that may look OK initially, but will not last. Before long, the paint may start cracking, chipping, and/or peeling, requiring another paint job after first removing all of the old paint.

## Avoiding Body Shop Rip-offs

Beware of shops that offer to "save you the deductible" by cheating the insurance company. That's insurance fraud, and if a shop is that dishonest, they'll probably cheat you, too.

Before accepting a repaired vehicle, be sure to do a thorough inspection of all repaired and painted areas—in the sunlight. Test drive the vehicle to make sure it runs OK, and don't accept a vehicle that is not completely finished.

Check the final invoice against the original estimate to verify that all the parts were installed and the repairs were done. Don't accept a final invoice unless all labor and parts are itemized, and all used or non-OEM parts are identified on the invoice.

## Consumers' Rights vs. Insurance Companies

Most insurance companies will try to steer consumers to one of the body shops on their "preferred" list, which basically consists of shops that are willing to repair cars for less money. With such a heavy emphasis on lower costs, there are legitimate concerns over the quality of repairs. Attempts may also be made to use aftermarket parts instead of original equipment—again, to save money.

In most states, insurance companies cannot force consumers to use their preferred shops or to have aftermarket parts installed instead of original equipment, unless those terms are spelled out in the insurance policy. Likewise, a motorist can't force an insurance company to pay whatever they demand to repair a vehicle, so some sort of middle ground needs to be found.

A fair compromise—one that's usually acceptable for disputes between two parties in small claims court—is for the consumer to get three estimates from shops of his choice, then the insurance company pays the amount of the lowest estimate. (The insurance company, however, may not think this is fair.)

Consumers who want top-quality repairs using original equipment parts may have to fight their insurance company to get their way, but they also have a right to have their vehicle restored to the condition it was in before a collision. And the previous condition probably didn't include cheap parts and poor-quality installation.

So be prepared to stand up for your rights, and remember that insurance companies are regulated by states, so complaints about them can be filed with the state insurance commissioner. For extreme cases of misconduct by an insurance company (refusing to pay claims, etc.), consult a local attorney about possible legal action.

# 11

# Smog & Safety Inspections

Mandatory inspections for safety or smog equipment present motorists with a real dilemma. Few states have centralized testing by shops that don't do any repairs, so most inspections are done by shops that are more than happy to perform any "necessary" repairs uncovered during an inspection.

Vehicles that fail inspections are required to be fixed (with few exceptions). Failure to comply often results in cancelled or unrenewed registration, tickets, and in some cases the vehicle may be impounded. Since the shops and mechanics are licensed by the state to perform the inspections, motorists usually assume that inspections and recommended repairs are legitimate. However, that is often not the case.

# SAFETY INSPECTIONS

Annual safety inspections were originally designed to keep unsafe vehicles off the roads, thereby preventing accidents. Some have criticized the effectiveness and cost of running inspection programs, while others claim that they are beneficial and should be mandatory in more states. Inspections have been required in 21 states for over two decades, but that number is not expected to grow due to lack of pressure by the federal government. (The number has actually dropped—there were 31 states with safety inspections thirty years ago.)

Safety inspections have turned out to be quite popular among many of the repair shops that inspect cars. Why? Because of the opportunity to make extra money. State laws have limited the inspection fees in many cases, making it difficult to profit from performing basic inspections, so the big money is in selling additional repairs (whether they're really needed or not).

## Faulty Inspections

Unnecessary repairs are often sold as a result of safety inspections, but intentional overselling does not deserve all the blame. Incompetence is a major problem in the auto repair industry and it is responsible for a lot of the unnecessary repairs that are performed. There is, however, a lot of auto repair fraud going on, and whether your hard-earned money is lost due to fraud or incompetence, the end result is still the same—your money is gone.

Besides exposing motorists to the risk of unnecessary repairs, safety inspections can also give drivers a false sense of security by implying (or stating) that a vehicle is safe, when in fact serious safety defects had been missed. Incompetent mechanics who fail to discover safety problems endanger the lives of those in an unsafe vehicle, as well as other motorists around them. The following story suggests that fraudulent and/or incompetent inspections may be commonplace—the 10 shops that were busted were selected at random from the phone book.

In 1992 the Pennsylvania Attorney General sued 10 Midas Muffler shops in the Pittsburgh area after an undercover investigation was done. A female detective posing as a customer visited the shops, asking for a safety inspection at each one. Three of the Midas shops were charged with issuing inspection stickers after failing to detect needed repairs and all 10 were charged with failing to note serious safety defects. Some of them were also charged with recommending unnecessary repairs.

## SMOG INSPECTIONS

Under the federal Clean Air Act, 98 cities across the country with moderate smog levels are required to have basic emissions inspection and maintenance programs, also known as "I/M" programs. Another 82 cities with more serious smog problems are required to have "enhanced I/M" programs that use a dynamometer to simulate actual driving conditions during the emissions test. As other cities increase in population (and cars), causing higher levels of air pollution, they will also be added to the list.

In the past, most emissions tests were done by shops that also performed repairs, similar to the safety inspections mentioned earlier. With thousands of repair shops available to do the tests, many competed for business by lowering their prices or offering "pass-or-no-pay" inspections, creating bargains for some lucky motorists. Other shops competed in more creative ways.

## Widespread Fraud

Investigations conducted by several states revealed widespread fraud in the inspection programs administered by private "test-and-repair" shops. Too many cars that should have failed were being passed, and many motorists were being sold unnecessary repairs as a result of faulty or fraudulent inspections.

In California, an investigation in the mid-1980s revealed that shops were failing to identify missing or altered smog equipment during 60-80% of the inspections. Some shops would pass cars with excessive emissions or missing smog equipment as a favor to regular customers (or to encourage people to recommend the shop to their friends), some would issue illegal inspection certificates for money (bribes), and some routinely passed cars that should have failed because of gross incompetence.

Due to widespread fraud in that state's inspection program, the California Bureau of Automotive Repair was authorized in 1986 to issue citations and collect fines from offending shops. After eleven months of undercover runs, the Bureau had issued citations to 437 shops and collected $130,750 in fines. Undercover operations increased, with more shops being caught every year. In 1992 alone, the Bureau issued 986 citations and collected fines totaling $435,250.

Shops that routinely issued illegal smog certificates (known as "cert-mills") were targeted by the Bureau. In a one-year period, over 100 shops were busted for smog fraud; the results: shops were shut down, owners and mechanics were arrested and sentenced to jail.

Some shops were providing used-car dealers with thousands of illegal smog certificates; over two dozen dealers were also arrested. In one 1992 raid on 28 shops in the Los Angeles area, 49 mechanics and/or owners were arrested and charged with felonies. Of those, 39 were convicted and sentenced to an average jail term of 144 days.

By 1992, California's "faulty inspection" rate had dropped to 15% after numerous changes were made to their inspection program. In addition to the increased undercover operations, mechanics were required to take tougher tests and shops were required to have more sophisticated equipment. Air pollution in California had actually been reduced 19% (from 20 years ago), an achievement that was still short of the federally mandated 25% reduction. But the fraud continued.

## New Smog Programs & Centralized Testing

Fraudulent smog inspections were not limited to California; they were such a widespread problem that the EPA wanted to eliminate all inspections by private garages. Their position was that "test-and-repair" shops could not be trusted to honestly and competently perform inspections, so they wanted to see all testing done by centralized inspection stations, either run by the government or by one company. Due to intense lobbying on behalf of the thousands of shops that would be put out of business, the EPA did not get its way.

Exclusive centralized testing is still only used by a few states. Some use a combination of centralized and private shops, while the majority of states still use private shops for testing and repairs. In California, private shops will still be allowed to perform tests, repairs, and certification for about 85% of the cars. Enhanced I/M areas (those with the most serious air quality problems) will use centralized testing for the dirtiest cars—gross polluters, high-mileage fleet vehicles, and vehicles with tampered emissions systems.

New technology will play a big part in the smog programs of the future. To catch gross polluters that have somehow evaded the system, "remote sensors" can be used along freeway onramps and other busy roads, recording tailpipe emissions and license numbers. Letters can be sent to the registered owners of offending vehicles, instructing them to get an inspection at a centralized station (with penalties for not complying, of course).

Consumer reaction to the different smog programs has varied from mere complaints to outright anarchy, depending on what programs were introduced and how they were implemented. In some areas where centralized testing was started, long lines caused motorists to rebel. After thousands complained and refused to get inspections, one state's program was put on hold.

In California, the governor and the state legislature refused to implement the EPA's centralized testing program because it would have reduced the number of inspection stations from 9,000 to only 200. (That would have been a real nightmare in a state with over 20 million cars.) So the state was granted a waiver and now runs a modified EPA program using the existing test-and-repair stations, some centralized testing and remote sensors.

**Smog Inspection Scams**

Some of the typical smog inspection rip-offs include bait-and-switch advertising, low-ball estimates, intentionally failing a vehicle to sell unnecessary repairs, and charging inflated prices for additional repairs that may or may not be needed.

In the bait-and-switch scam, low prices are advertised to lure customers to the shop, with no intention of letting the majority actually get out for the advertised price. Numerous "problems" are invented as reasons to fail vehicles, with people being sold unnecessary air filters, spark plugs, tune-ups, timing or idle adjustments, fuel injection cleaning, carburetor overhauls, catalytic converters, etc.

Repairs that are sold may not even be done—since the customer is told, "your vehicle passed after we fixed it," most people don't suspect that they were ripped off. One obvious case of fraud involved a lady who was sold a carburetor overhaul so her car would pass; she fell for it, even though her car didn't even have a carburetor. (It had fuel injection.) Some people have paid for tune-ups when only one spark plug (or wire) was replaced, and many have been sold new converters that they didn't need.

"Low-balling" is the practice of quoting a dishonestly low estimate just to get a car in the shop. After the car is left at the shop—and usually disassembled—the customer receives a phone call with a higher "updated" estimate, which is really the true price that the shop knew about when they quoted the lower one. (This is a common scam for many types of auto repair.)

Some shops merely pretend to have low prices by advertising a few low-priced specials, creating the illusion that their overall prices are lower than others. Ads are often run comparing a low-priced special with the higher regular prices charged by dealers or other shops. However, the "cheaper" shop's prices for all other parts and services (that aren't part of the special) may be much higher than those charged by other shops. Since there's little or no profit in low-priced auto repair, there will be a lot of pressure on employees to sell a lot of the higher-priced additional parts and services.

**Faulty and Fraudulent Inspections**

Part of the fraudulent smog problem lies with consumers who insist on mechanics passing cars even though they should fail. If a mechanic doesn't offer to pass a vehicle for a bribe, customers will sometimes make the suggestion. After motorists learned that repairs could cost hundreds of dollars, many mechanics have been told, "I know it needs a lot of work, but here's $50 (or $100)—just give me a smog certificate anyway." In some areas, motorists who do this are subject to fines as high as $2,500. The mechanic can be fined $5,000 and might even get a jail term.

Aside from the moral and legal aspects of encouraging illegal inspections, there are also potential mechanical problems that can end up costing far more in the long run. A vehicle that is not properly maintained and repaired can end up becoming a gross polluter that will someday have to be repaired—with no cost limit—or taken off the streets. Partial repairs (doing as little as possible to pass a vehicle) can cause more expensive damage to other components, resulting in a larger repair bill several weeks or months after the "band-aid" repair is done.

Faulty partial repairs often happen because of incompetence. For example, a mechanic who is not highly skilled or properly trained may replace a failed catalytic converter, temporarily cleaning up the exhaust enough to pass inspection, without detecting the other problems that caused the converter to fail. (It's rare for a converter to fail on a car that has no other problems.) Six months later, the new converter fails again, but it's out of warranty. So the customer has to pay another $300-500 plus the cost of fixing the original problem that ruined two converters.

Any money spent on faulty inspections and repairs may be wasted if a vehicle is later caught and labeled as a "gross polluter" or a "tampered vehicle" (one with missing, modified, or disconnected emission equipment). In those cases, cost limits may not apply—complete repairs may be required, no matter how much they cost.

Between random smog checks, remote sensors, and the expanding biennial inspection programs, it's going to be a lot harder to drive a "dirty" car without getting caught, so motorists should just have the repairs done properly. If everyone does this, we'll all breathe easier.

## Specialty Shops & Chain Stores— Are They Really "Experts"?

Are specialty shops (tune-up, smog & tune, tune & lube, etc.) and well-known chain stores better than other types of shops for smog inspections? Not necessarily. All types of shops have had smog busts—including chain stores and specialty shops—so consumers would be wise to do their homework before choosing a shop. Look for a clean track record and well-trained technicians.

One major negative for low-priced specialty shops is their tendency to have mostly lower-paid, less-skilled mechanics. (I'm being charitable here; many of them are just parts changers, not mechanics.) As they gain experience and training, they usually leave for other better-paying jobs. Once again, their replacements are typically lower-paid trainees.

The owner of a large lube, tune and smog chain recently complained about the new legal requirements in his state. If they want to continue doing smog inspections, they'll have to get new equipment and either hire better mechanics or spend a lot of money training the ones they already have. The owner was whining about the cost of hiring better mechanics; he also said that if his mechanics received a lot more training, he would have to pay them a lot more—or they would leave.

Performing a lot of smog inspections or tune-ups does not make someone an expert; education, training, intelligence and advanced test equipment are all necessary. To be an "emissions system expert" requires one to also be a driveability/computer/fuel injection expert, and they're in demand because their numbers are few. They're also able to command high salaries, as much as $50,000 (or more) per year in major cities, so you're not likely to find one working in a low-priced tune-up or smog shop.

## Smog Busts—
## Specialty Shops & Chain Stores

The following list shows the number of citations and fines against specialty shops and major chains for faulty or fraudulent smog inspections—*in California alone*. The citations were issued between 9/1/90 and 12/31/91 as a result of undercover investigations and carried fines ranging from $250 to $1,500 each. Some of the shops were closed after their licenses were revoked.

Econo Lube N Tune—57
Firestone Auto Centers—31
Goodyear Auto Centers—12
Precision Tune—12
Quality Tune Up—18
Sears Auto Centers—16
Smog Pros—56
Speedee Oil Change & Tune Up—13
Tuneup Masters—32

For most of those companies, the violations slowed to a trickle the following year (1992). A few still received a lot of citations and fines that year:

Econo Lube N Tune—30
Smog Pros—21
Tuneup Masters—12

**Free Repairs—**
**Manufacturers Emission System Warranties**

Motorists whose vehicles receive failing grades after smog inspections may be eligible for free repairs under a manufacturer's emission system warranty. Of course, vehicles with missing, modified, or disconnected smog equipment are not eligible for free repairs, but all other vehicles that fall within the time and mileage limits qualify. These warranties are not limited to just the original owners—they apply to all current owners of vehicles that qualify, so be sure to check into them before paying for any emission system repairs.

On pre-1990 cars & light-to-medium-duty trucks, repair or replacement of defective emission-related parts is covered for 5 years or 50,000 miles.

On 1990 & newer cars, light-duty trucks & medium-duty vehicles, all repairs and adjustments necessary to make a vehicle pass inspection—including the retest—are covered for 3 years or 50,000 miles. Also, repair or replacement of certain high-priced defective parts (listed in owner's manual) is covered for 7 years or 70,000 miles.

For all heavy-duty gasoline-powered trucks, repair or replacement of defective emission-related parts is covered for 5 years or 50,000 miles.

# HOW TO AVOID INSPECTION RIP-OFFS

First, to prevent the surprise of facing steep repair bills after failing an inspection, make sure your vehicle is properly maintained by a well-trained technician. This will not only increase the chances of passing inspections, but it can also tip you off that recommended repairs may not be necessary.

141

Where should you go for inspections? If you have a choice, my advice is to find the best shop, with the smartest mechanics, and go to them for everything—don't shop around looking for bargains. If you have to go to another shop for an inspection, don't let them do any repairs; go back to your mechanic for a second opinion.

In choosing a shop, look for a good track record (by checking with your local Better Business Bureau or state consumer protection agency) and check the qualifications of their mechanics.

If you see a shop that runs a lot of low-priced ads, that's usually a good indication that they have some type of sales commission or quota to encourage the sale of additional repairs. And be wary of shops that say you need a new catalytic converter—especially if your vehicle is in good shape. Dishonest shops love to sell new converters because they get $400 to $500 for a job that takes less than 20 minutes.

Finally, when in doubt, always get a second (or third) opinion before giving authorization for any major repairs.

# 12

# Lube & Oil Shops

Shops specializing in "fast and cheap" lube and oil services have become very popular in recent years. The convenience and low prices are appealing, but problems and abuses have occurred at some of these shops in the past, so consumers should exercise caution when using them.

There are two types of lube and oil shops: The first type only does basic maintenance such as lubrication, oil changes and filters; the second type does tune-ups, smog inspections and other repairs in addition to lube and oil changes. This chapter covers the first type, shops that only perform basic maintenance. For information on the others, see Chapter 4, "Tune-up Shops."

Most lube and oil shops are franchises, which means that a parent company lends its name and sets up the business for someone who is willing to pay a franchise fee. A background in service (or repair) of motor vehicles is usually not required, so many franchisees have little or no experience in this area. While it is true that performing lube and oil changes does not require a great amount of skill or education, and the parent company usually provides some training for the new owner, the lack of automotive experience can sometimes cause problems.

Since lube and oil shops are performing this service at prices that are usually much lower than those charged by repair shops, many of them are forced to hire inexperienced workers who will work for low wages. And this is where the danger lies: Many of the employees doing the lube and oil changes have no prior experience in servicing motor vehicles.

Workers are often under pressure to sell additional filters and other services while still completing the lube and oil change in 10-15 minutes, resulting in mistakes being made when a worker has to choose between doing a job well and doing it quickly. To save time, some workers have installed incorrect oil filters because they did not have the correct one in stock, and oil drain plugs that did not tighten properly were not repaired, causing leaks.

A number of "fast and cheap" lube and oil shops have caused serious damage to customers' vehicles, some so severe that engines had to be completely rebuilt or replaced. Even though it was their negligence that caused the engine damage, the shops didn't pay the entire cost of the overhauls. They prorated the customers' share of the bills based on vehicle mileage, so the victims ended up paying hundreds (or thousands) of dollars for an engine overhaul after bringing their vehicle in for a simple, "inexpensive" oil change. (And those were the ones who could prove that the shops caused the damage. Others weren't so lucky.)

Some of the mistakes made by workers at lube and oil shops include: failure to tighten oil drain plugs, improper installation of oil filters, failure to repair leaking oil drain plugs, use of incorrect fluids and filters, and failure to put the proper amount of oil in engines. Since a typical lube and oil shop needs to service at least 35 vehicles per day to be profitable, mistakes such as these are not that unusual. (I was told that a major lube and oil chain has had a large number of damaged engines and insurance claims caused by incompetent workers in their shops.)

Some lube shops have expanded into other services, including air conditioning, automatic transmissions, and smog inspections, creating even more problems. The low-paid, low-skilled workers in lube and oil shops are not mechanics, so avoid using them for anything other than oil changes.

Another problem area is the use of inexpensive, low-quality parts. Although virtually all lube and oil shops use name-brand motor oil, not all use high-quality, name-brand oil filters and air filters. Using inexpensive filters—*especially oil filters*—is risky because many of them do not provide the same protection as name-brand parts. Trying to save a dollar or two on a filter can result in increased engine wear and premature engine failure. *Insist on high-quality, name-brand parts.*

Putting the wrong fluid in a vehicle is another potential problem area for these shops. Due to the high-volume business that is done by most of them, fluids are usually bought and stored in bulk quantities, and hose reels are used to dispense most fluids. If the hoses containing different fluids look the same, the wrong fluid may be put in your vehicle by an inexperienced or distracted worker. Many shops have color-coded hoses to prevent this from happening. Make sure the hoses used for dispensing fluids are clearly marked.

Brake fluid should not be stored and dispensed out of large barrels or other containers because the fluid will absorb moisture from the air and become contaminated. The use of contaminated brake fluid will cause rust or corrosion to form inside the brake cylinders and calipers, resulting in premature brake failure. Make sure the brake fluid is stored and dispensed out of small containers (one gallon or less).

## Lube & Oil Guidelines

Lube and oil shops can be a convenient and inexpensive resource for servicing your vehicle—if some guidelines are followed. Some shops are professionally run, but since most of these shops are franchises with different owners, even those under the same name may not provide the same level of service. If you decide to use a lube and oil shop, be sure to check it out first.

Look for shops with workers who are certified. The Automotive Oil Change Association (formerly the National Association of Independent Lubes) provides testing and certification for independent shops. Testing and certification for the major chains (and franchises) is provided by the Convenient Automotive Service Institute.

Ask how much experience the workers have; if they just started working there, ask for someone with more experience. Don't go to a brand-new lube and oil shop until they've been open for several weeks. (When a new one first opens for business, most of the workers will usually be inexperienced. Let them practice on someone else's car before you allow them to touch yours.)

Make sure they use high-quality, name-brand parts, and beware of shops that try to sell air filters, breather elements, or other items every time the oil is changed. Depending on driving conditions, those items normally last at least 10-15,000 miles.

Look for a clean, well-organized shop; avoid ones that look like a "three-ring circus." *And finally, to be safe, check for leaks after they're done.*

# 13

## Avoiding Rip-offs; Getting Your Money Back

To avoid rip-offs, use the information in this book to locate a reputable shop that has well-trained, highly skilled technicians. (See Chapter 15, "Finding Mechanics You Can Trust.") However, that may not always be possible, so the following information is provided to help consumers avoid paying for unnecessary repairs.

If you have to take your vehicle to an unfamiliar shop, or if you just haven't found a reputable shop yet, be suspicious of anyone using scare tactics or other pressure to sell expensive additional repairs. Honest shops don't operate that way. All of the good shops that I have run across have the same attitude: If a customer doesn't seem interested in repairs that a shop is recommending, the shop should just note the recommendations on the customer's repair order and drop the subject.

Getting all recommendations in writing *before* repairs are authorized is a good way to avoid some rip-offs. If a shop says that a repair is "needed," tell them to put that in writing first—and to save your old parts because you want to take them with you. That might discourage some shops from selling an unnecessary repair. If they won't say—in writing—that a repair is "needed," it's probably something that can wait, maybe for years.

Also, watch out for statements like "we recommend (or suggest) the following repairs;" that's a common trick that's used to sell unnecessary parts and services. And be on the lookout for shops that use the word "needed" to get your authorization, then write up the repair as a "recommended/suggested" one on the repair order. (If the shop is recommending a legitimate "preventive maintenance" repair, they should be able to show you why a particular part should be replaced before it actually fails.)

Use common sense to determine whether repairs are urgently needed or not. *Don't be fooled by scare tactics!* If you weren't experiencing any problems before you brought your vehicle to the shop, it probably wouldn't hurt to put off any major repairs for a day or two (while you get a second opinion).

However, if you're shown something like a cracked brake hose, a brake fluid leak or some other safety problem, then you may need to have a repair done immediately. Just be sure to get your old parts back in case you want to have them checked by another shop.

Before you authorize additional parts or services, tell the shop to show you what's wrong. Compare your parts with new ones so you can see how bad they are. If the parts don't look bad to you, but the mechanic claims they are, don't get into an argument with him. Just say that you can't have any more work done at this time and they will have to put your vehicle back together so you can drive it home. (Then you can take it to another shop for a second opinion.)

A difficult situation can arise if the shop claims they can't put your vehicle back together without installing the new parts they've been trying to sell you. When this happens, you have several choices: demand to speak to the owner/manager, threaten to call the local/state consumer protection agency *and the police*, tell them you're going to file complaints with the Better Business Bureau, have your vehicle towed to another shop (while it's still apart), or pay for the additional repairs.

**Getting Your Money Back**

If you can't convince the manager to put your vehicle back together without the new parts, and you don't want to have your vehicle towed to another shop, tell them to go ahead with the additional repairs. *Make sure they put all of your old parts in the trunk, then pay for the repairs with a credit card—don't pay with cash or a check.*

You may be told that you can't have your old parts back because you were sold rebuilt ones at "exchange" prices, but this is only true if you don't pay the "core charge" on the parts. Pay the extra charge, if necessary, so you can have your old parts back. (The law states that repair shops must return old parts to consumers when requested, so don't let them tell you that you can't have them back.)

Without your old parts, you won't be able to prove that you were sold unnecessary repairs. After the dispute is settled, or you discover that the repairs really were necessary, you can return the parts for a refund of the core charge.

Take your old parts to a reputable repair shop (a new-car dealership that sells the same make of car would be ideal), then ask them if the parts look like they came from your car and whether they needed to be replaced. There may be a small charge for this, but it's worth it for your peace of mind; also, if it turns out that replacement wasn't necessary, another shop's statement will be helpful in getting your money back. *Get their statements in writing.*

If several mechanics tell you that it wasn't necessary to replace those parts, or (worse yet) that the parts the shop supposedly replaced didn't come from your car, call the shop and ask to speak to the owner or manager. Tell him that you had the old parts checked out, that you were told they didn't need to be replaced, and you want your money back.

If the manager refuses to refund your money, tell him that you are going to notify the credit card company that you have a dispute with the shop and that you refuse to pay that charge before the dispute is settled.

## The Demand Letter

Go home and write a letter to the shop owner or manager, repeating your demand for a refund, as well as the reasons why you think you are entitled to one. (Be sure to include a deadline: "If you do not refund part/all of my money by [date], I will notify the credit card company to refuse payment and I will take you to small claims court.") Make several copies of the demand letter, then send it by registered mail for proof that it was received.

It's very important to follow these instructions carefully. The old parts, the statements from other mechanics, and the demand letter are all needed to refuse payment on your credit card or take the shop to court, so make sure they are done in the proper order.

Don't tell the shop that you intend to refuse payment on your credit card until *after* you have picked up your car and had the old parts checked by another shop. A shop that knows ahead of time that you are going to refuse payment may insist that you pay cash before they let you pick up your car. If this happens, you may never get your money back, even if you take them to court and win. (It's not easy to collect on a judgment if they don't feel like paying you.)

When you refuse to pay for a particular charge on your credit card statement because of a dispute with a merchant, the credit card company does a "charge back" against that shop's account for the disputed amount. This must be done *before* you pay the disputed amount on your credit card statement.

Make sure you've had the old parts checked and sent the demand letter before payment is due on your credit card. If you haven't done both of those things yet, you may have to make a minimum payment on the disputed amount, but *don't pay the entire amount.*

After you have verified that the old parts didn't need to be replaced and sent the demand letter, notify the card company (in writing) that you have a dispute with the shop and that you refuse to pay that charge.

*If you do refuse payment on your credit card account, the shop may take you to court,* especially if they think you have no grounds for a refund. However, if the shop has sold you unnecessary repairs and you've followed the above procedure, the shop owner will know he's going to lose, so he probably won't sue. Even if the shop doesn't file suit, the vehicle owner may choose to sue the shop in small claims court to resolve the dispute and to make it a public record.

Using a credit card to avoid paying for unnecessary repairs is only effective on fairly simple repairs such as brakes, minor tune-ups, and front end work, because it's easy to verify whether the parts needed to be replaced. If you go to low-priced shops in spite of what you have learned in this book, it would be a good idea to protect yourself using a credit card. However, it's not easy (or cost effective) to test carburetors, computers, or other electrical parts after they have been removed from the vehicle, so this procedure won't usually work on complex repairs.

Before using this strategy, read the section on your credit card statement that explains your rights and restrictions. This is usually permitted for purchases over $50 that are made in your home state or within 100 miles of your mailing address. These restrictions may not apply if the credit card issuer owns or operates the repair shop.

The "save-your-parts" and "demand-letter" strategy may also be used if you paid by check when you were ripped off, but you'll have to go to small claims court to get your money back if the shop is not cooperative. (And there's no guarantee that you'll collect if you win.) That's why I recommend using a credit card to pay for all repairs. Also, in some parts of the country, stopping payment on a check may be against the law, so don't try this without knowing whether it's legal or not.

## Dispute Mediation or Arbitration

Many repair shops (for example, all AAA Approved Repair Facilities and most new-car dealership service departments) have arbitration procedures in place that can eliminate the need for expensive and time-consuming court cases. Decisions are usually binding on the shop only, giving the consumer the right to take his case to court if he doesn't think the decision was fair. Be sure to ask if this service is available.

# 14

# Agencies: Who to Call

## AUTO REPAIR COMPLAINTS

### CALIFORNIA--
Bureau of Automotive Repair
10240 Systems Parkway
Sacramento, CA 95827
Calif. only  (800) 952-5210
All others   (916) 445-1254

### MICHIGAN--
Bureau of Automotive Regulation
208 N. Capitol Ave.
Lansing, MI 48918
Mich. only  (800) 292-4204
All others    (517) 373-7416

### ALL OTHER STATES--
Contact your state's consumer protection agency
or the attorney general's office.

For complaints against auto repair shops, call or write the appropriate agency for your state. Complaint forms can usually be requested by phone. Action can be taken for obvious violations of a state's laws or regulations. If numerous complaints are filed against one shop, an investigation may be started.

Complaints can also be made to the local city/county district attorney's consumer protection division and the Better Business Bureau.


## FACTORY RECALLS, SAFETY DEFECTS & SERVICE BULLETINS--

National Highway Traffic Safety Administration
400 7th Street SW, Room 5110
Washington, DC 20590
(800) 424-9393

The NHTSA collects information on all automotive recalls (including child safety seats), safety defects and complaints, crash tests, standards for all automotive parts, and factory service bulletins covering all vehicles sold in the United States. Will research service bulletins (for a fee) to locate those explaining a manufacturer's solution to a difficult repair problem. Has certified data and films on crash tests.

Factory service bulletin information can also be obtained (for a fee) by calling the following manufacturers' toll-free customer service numbers.

GM (800) 551-4123;  FORD (800) 241-3673;
AUDI, CHRYSLER, NISSAN, VW (800) 544-8021.

If you need to get recall or service bulletin information immediately, any repair shop with an Alldata computerized information system can print them out for you (typical charge: $10 to $15). To locate a shop near you, call Alldata Corp. at (800) 829-8727, select "operator."

## SECRET WARRANTIES, VEHICLE DEFECTS, SAFETY RECALLS & LEMON LAWS--

Center for Auto Safety
2001 S Street NW, Suite 410
Washington, DC 20009
(202) 328-7700

The Center for Auto Safety is a nonprofit clearing house for information on secret warranties, vehicle defects, recalls, lemon laws and attorney referral to lemon law specialists. To receive information, send a self-addressed, stamped envelope to the Center with a note listing the year, make and model of your vehicle. Don't forget to specify what kind of information you need. (Normal response time is 3 to 4 weeks.)

## EMISSION WARRANTIES--

Environmental Protection Agency
401 M Street SW
Washington, DC 20460
(202) 260-2090

The EPA has information on all vehicle emission warranties, gas mileage data for all vehicles, and import/export emission information.

155

## MEDIATION & ARBITRATION--

Autocap
National Automobile Dealers Association
8400 Westpark Drive
McLean, VA 22102
(703) 821-7144

Third party mediation for anything related to vehicle manufacturers or dealers. Arbitration is also available for unresolved problems.

———————————

Better Business Bureau (BBB),
American Automobile Association (AAA)

The Better Business Bureau and AAA also have arbitration programs for some manufacturers, dealers and repair shops. Contact your local BBB or AAA office for details.

# 15

# Finding Mechanics
# You Can Trust

How can you tell which repair shops or mechanics can be trusted to give you an honest deal? It's the best-equipped shops with the smartest mechanics, the ones repairing cars that other shops can't fix. Ignore those sleazy, low-priced ads, and look for the guys who get paid for their brains instead of their sales ability.

Before you take your vehicle to any shop, find out how they measure up. The following guidelines are provided to help you find the best shops; if possible, *all* of the categories below should be considered before a final decision is made.

## EDUCATION

The most important consideration should be the education or skill level of the mechanic, based on studying and continuing education classes, not on years of experience. The experience gained from working on cars in the 1960s or 1970s is all but worthless today because 1980-98 vehicles do not even resemble those built 20 or 30 years ago.

An unskilled (i.e., uneducated) mechanic will make a lot more mistakes than an educated one, and he will have to charge his customers for most of his mistakes if he wants to stay in business. For this reason, the consumer has the best chance of not being charged for unnecessary repairs by finding an educated mechanic.

There are several ways to determine a mechanic's level of education. If you are at the repair shop, look on the walls of the office or customer waiting room for certificates and/or licenses that the mechanic has earned. Most community colleges and trade schools issue certificates to mechanics verifying that they have completed a particular course in auto repair. A regular pattern of attendance (at least two or three courses every year) shows that a mechanic is at least trying to keep up with the latest technology. A mechanic who hasn't taken a class in years will not have the knowledge required to properly diagnose and repair late-model vehicles.

Ask the mechanic (or shop owner) what schools or classes he attends, and what trade publications he reads, to keep up with the changing technology. If he says he is able to keep up without going to school or studying, you should look for another mechanic; it's no longer possible for a mechanic to figure out (by himself) everything he needs to know to work on the computer-controlled vehicles built after 1980.

A mechanic's library of repair manuals and other reference books can also be used to indicate his level of education or skill. The average shop repairing the most common domestic and import vehicles needs to buy at least seven or eight manuals every year, so if a shop has been in business for ten years and only has ten or fifteen manuals, I would suspect that the mechanic either hates to read or is not willing to invest the money required to have up-to-date information. Unless you're driving a really old car (twenty-plus years), a shop that doesn't have a lot of books will not be able to properly repair your car.

The manuals used by the most well-trained, highly skilled technicians are those published by the vehicle manufacturers, and also by Mitchell and Motor. Manuals published by other companies are mostly for "do-it-yourself" mechanics, as they are not usually comprehensive enough for the professional. If a mechanic's library consists mainly of (small) books published by other companies, that can be an indication that he's not very knowledgeable.

Ask the mechanic or shop owner what they do when a vehicle has a problem, and they can't figure it out because everything looks and tests OK. (If he says that never happens, head for the nearest exit—he's lying, because it happens all the time.) Every shop should have a comprehensive set of technical service bulletins (at least 600-700 pages every year), or at least have access to them through a call-in service.

Many late-model vehicles (especially those with computer controls) develop problems that are impossible to diagnose and repair using normal test equipment and procedures. The vehicle manufacturers know these problems exist, so they publish technical service bulletins that explain how to solve them. If a shop doesn't have access to these bulletins, they will be making incorrect guesses when diagnosing many problems, and the vehicle owner will end up paying for unnecessary repairs.

Several fairly new computer systems (by Alldata Corporation and Mitchell International) have been made especially for repair shops. These systems have most of the repair manuals, labor guides, wiring diagrams, and technical service bulletins on computer disks (CDs) for easy reference. A shop with one of these systems won't need very many books, since they contain over 200,000 printed pages.

## MECHANIC CERTIFICATION

Look for ASE-certified mechanics. "ASE" is the symbol of the National Institute for Automotive Service Excellence, which is a voluntary, national testing program created to help the public identify shops employing knowledgeable mechanics. Certification is not a guarantee that a mechanic is honest or even highly proficient, but it does show that the mechanic is reasonably intelligent and understands the automotive categories that he is certified in.

The ASE tests are difficult enough to weed out at least 50% of the mechanics taking them for the first time; many mechanics refuse to take them at all because they don't like taking tests (and are afraid they won't pass). Less than 10% of all mechanics in the country are ASE-certified.

I have taken and passed a number of ASE tests, and can testify that they are not that difficult for a technician who is literate and knows his trade. However, they will definitely eliminate someone who does not have a good understanding of automotive diagnosis and repair.

Don't assume all of the mechanics working in a repair shop are certified in all categories just because the shop displays the ASE symbol. To use the symbol, a shop is only required to have one mechanic who is ASE-certified in one out of eight areas.

When you take your vehicle in for repairs, insist that an ASE-certified technician do all of the work (except for lube and oil changes). If more people would do this, it would encourage shop owners to employ only certified technicians.

The ASE program is excellent, but it does fall short in one area: testing for theory and knowledge concerning engine performance on computer-controlled vehicles. Most of the manufacturers started installing computers in their vehicles between 1979 and 1984, so a mechanic without a thorough understanding of computer systems will not be able to properly diagnose and repair driveability problems on most late-model vehicles.

Until the ASE program begins testing for knowledge of computer system theory, consumers will have to evaluate a mechanic's level of education and skill in this area, using the guidelines mentioned earlier in this chapter.

Almost all new-car dealerships employ ASE-certified mechanics, as do many large independent repair shops and chains. Look for the "ASE" symbol in shop advertisements, signs, and patches worn by the mechanics.

## QUALITY PARTS

The use of inexpensive parts will almost always result in premature failure, which is not only expensive because the repair did not last as long as it should have, but it can be dangerous if it causes brake failure or stalling in the middle of an intersection or a railroad crossing.

Ask the shop owner what brands of parts they use for brakes, tune ups, electrical (starters, alternators, regulators, etc.), and engine parts—even gaskets. Make sure they are using high-quality, name-brand parts; if you don't recognize the brands he mentions, call an auto parts store that is used by professional mechanics and ask if the brands mentioned are of high quality. (The easiest way to find the name of a good local auto parts store is to call a dealership parts department and ask them for a recommendation.)

*Beware of "look-alike" parts,* as well as the repair shops that use them. Low-quality, counterfeit parts that resemble name brands are often sold to shops for a fraction of the price of high-quality parts. The boxes that the counterfeit parts come in often use the same designs and colors as those containing name brands, so they appear to be high-quality parts to the uninformed.

Some shop owners buy these look-alike parts through the mail from out-of-state telephone solicitors, installing them in their customers' vehicles and charging the same prices that the name brands sell for. By doing this, a shop's profit margin on parts can be 50-70% instead of the normal 25-30%.

Insist on the use of high-quality, name-brand parts when your vehicle is repaired. Trying to save money on a brake job by using inexpensive parts can result in injury or even death if the brakes do not work properly. Since labor charges are now the major part of the typical repair bill, the use of inexpensive parts will not save money in the long run because the repair will not last as long as it should. The cheaper parts usually fail after the warranty expires, leaving the customer to pay the full cost of doing the repair over again.

## QUALITY DIAGNOSTIC & REPAIR WORK

If you want honest, high-quality diagnostic and repair work done on your vehicle, expect to pay for it. Because there's a shortage of well-trained, highly skilled technicians, it's not likely that a shop can find or keep one without paying him a lot of money. In many areas of the country with a high cost of living, a highly skilled technician can make at least $20 per hour. Add the cost of benefits to his salary and the total cost to a shop may be $25 per hour (or more).

In addition, a typical shop needs a minimum of $100,000 in equipment to work on late-model vehicles. Equipment payments, rent, utilities, insurance, office personnel and other expenses can easily add at least $15 to $20 to a shop's hourly overhead. And if overhead costs a repair shop $45 per hour (before the owner gets paid), they certainly can't afford to work on customers' vehicles without charging for everything they do.

Ask the shop if they charge for all diagnostic work, even if they end up doing the repairs. A professional shop will not only charge for all diagnostic work, but will refuse to repair a vehicle without first performing diagnostic tests to make sure the repair is necessary.

*Beware of shops that offer free diagnostics.* If a shop knows they are not going to be paid for any of the time spent diagnosing a problem, they will not want to spend much time checking it out. This will almost always result in unnecessary repairs because the shop will be more inclined to guess what is wrong instead of testing to pinpoint the problem. Today's vehicles are so complex that most problems require a minimum of one-half hour for an accurate diagnosis, with many electrical and computer problems requiring several hours.

Choosing a repair shop because it promises low prices is not a good idea for several reasons. First, low prices are often advertised (or dishonestly quoted over the phone) to get people into the shop, all for the purpose of selling them a lot of high-priced (or unnecessary) repairs.

Second, a shop may have lower prices because it employs less-skilled mechanics, because it doesn't have up-to-date equipment, or because it uses lower-quality parts than a shop charging higher prices. And the repair work of all shops (and even mechanics) is not of the same quality; some just want to finish the job as fast as possible,

163

while others are more concerned about turning out high-quality repairs.

A mechanic who is in a hurry is far more likely to overlook something that could cause a problem. If he has to choose between finishing a job quickly and interrupting it to obtain customer approval for additional parts and/or labor, he will usually choose to finish the job quickly. This practice often results in a repair that does not last as long as it should have, with the customer picking up the tab later on when the repair needs to be done over again (after the warranty expires, of course).

Generally speaking, shops with lower prices tend to put more emphasis on getting the job done quickly, and mechanics who are always in a hurry are more likely to make mistakes that the customer will end up paying for.

**REFERENCES**

Asking friends to recommend a shop can be a good starting point, but it's not foolproof. Why not? Because there are a lot of bad mechanics out there with loyal customers who mistakenly believe that the shop is giving them a fair deal. To make matters worse, those deceived customers are recommending those shops to all their friends. If you do ask your friends for a recommendation, make sure the shop meets all the other standards listed in this chapter.

And if the shop (or mechanic) that you've been using fails any of these categories, especially the first three, resist the temptation to stay with the shop you know instead of finding a new one. Remember, an educated mechanic will make fewer mistakes that you'll end up paying for.

Checking references on a repair shop that neither you nor any of your friends have used before is fairly simple. Several methods can be used, depending on how fast you need the information. The quickest way to check the complaint history of a shop is to call the local Better Business Bureau.

The state Department of Consumer Affairs can also provide information on repair shop complaints, but they usually require that requests be made in writing. Look in the phone book under "state government" listings for the agency nearest you. (In California, call the state Bureau of Automotive Repair; in Michigan, call the state Bureau of Automotive Regulation.)

When looking up a shop's complaint history, keep this in mind: Any shop that's been in business for a while is bound to get a few complaints, but they shouldn't get a lot. And the ones they do get should be resolved promptly and fairly.

An excellent method of getting referrals for auto repair is to call the local AAA office, which will give out (over the phone) the names of several shops in your area that are AAA Approved Auto Repair facilities.

Before a shop can qualify as a AAA Approved facility, it must meet AAA's standards for qualified personnel, customer service, necessary tools and equipment, good reputation, shop appearance, and insurance. AAA checks references from previous customers (taken at random from the shop's files), requiring a favorable response from at least 85% of those questioned.

To be in the AAA program, a shop must be approved in the following areas: engine tune-up, brakes, electrical systems, minor engine repair, and either heating/air conditioning or tires/steering/suspension. Optional areas include: major engine repairs, automatic transmission, manual transmission, and diagnostic lane.

A major benefit of the AAA Approved Repair program is their binding arbitration policy, which can save a customer the time and expense of going to court to resolve a complaint. (This is only available to members.)

One of the conditions of AAA approval is that the shops must accept AAA's decision regarding complaints. Customers with a complaint against an approved shop are encouraged to let AAA resolve the problem.

After interviewing the customer and the mechanic, reviewing the estimate and repair order, and road testing the vehicle to determine how well the job was done, a AAA representative (with a background in the auto repair business) will decide how the problem should be resolved. He may tell the shop to refund part or all of the amount charged for the repair, or he may tell the customer that a refund is not justified. AAA's decision is binding on the repair facility, but not on the customer, who is free to take the shop to court if he is not satisfied with the decision.

If AAA decides against a shop and they refuse to refund the customer's money, AAA will pay the customer the amount that is owed. Since all of their shops agreed to honor AAA's decision as a condition of approval, a shop's refusal to refund a customer's money could cause them to be dropped from the program.

Because of this policy, if you are considering using a shop that was approved by AAA at one time but is not any longer, you should try to find out why they're not in the program anymore. Some shop owners have told customers that they voluntarily dropped out because they were "tired of the paperwork" or "it wasn't worth the trouble," when the truth is that AAA dropped them from the program because they had too many complaints and/ or refused to refund a customer's money.

Since the AAA program checks most of the categories listed in this chapter, it can be used as a shortcut instead of doing the checking yourself. However, AAA's examination of a shop may not be as thorough and critical as if you had done it yourself, especially in the areas of mechanics' education and certification.

AAA allows an "equivalent" to ASE certification and will approve a shop without certification if the shop agrees to obtain it within two testing periods. AAA does require a formal training system for keeping employees up-to-date, but does not specify what type of classes mechanics must attend or how often.

A major drawback to using the AAA shortcut, besides the education and certification issues, is that many reputable repair shops are not in their program and may be overlooked. Also, the AAA repair program is only operating in about 30 states at this time.

It should be emphasized that a AAA Approved Repair facility is not guaranteed to be perfect or even the best shop in town, but has simply met the minimum standards set by AAA. If you decide to use their program to locate a repair shop, I recommend that you get the names of at least three or four shops in your area from AAA, then use the standards outlined in this chapter to determine which shop is the best.

Here's a shortcut that can be used almost anywhere, so it's especially useful when you're traveling: Call one or two auto parts stores that cater to professionals (for example, Napa Auto Parts or Carquest Auto Parts stores) and ask them for advice. Tell them you're new in town and you need to know which shops are the best for tough electrical and computer problems on late-model vehicles. (That will tell you where the smartest mechanics are.)

## SHOP EQUIPMENT

A typical repair shop needs to have *at least* $100,000 in equipment and tools for proper diagnosis and repair of late-model vehicles in the areas of tune up, electrical, air conditioning, brakes and minor engine repair.

Without the proper equipment, a mechanic is forced to guess at the cause of the problem instead of testing for it, which almost always results in the customer paying for unnecessary repairs. Also, if a shop does not have easy access to the equipment required to do a thorough repair job, they will be more inclined to take shortcuts that result in a repair not lasting as long as it should.

For example, on some late-model computer-controlled vehicles, a malfunctioning alternator can cause erratic engine operation by affecting the computer. This can happen without causing the alternator light to come on or the battery to go dead, so the alternator would not normally be suspect. A mechanic can properly diagnose this problem in about 20 minutes using one of the new computerized engine analyzers (that sell for about $30,000).

Without that analyzer, several hours might be wasted, and the computer might be replaced unnecessarily before the problem is properly diagnosed. That is how a repair that should only cost $200 ends up being $400 or more.

If a shop does not have a brake lathe to resurface drums and rotors, they'll have to send them out to a machine shop. This situation often results in the mechanic deciding not to resurface the drums and/or rotors because he doesn't want to wait for them. Also, if the shop is doing a brake job over again (for free) to resolve a complaint, they may not want to pay to have the parts resurfaced.

Failure to resurface the drums and/or rotors when the brakes are relined often results in poor brake performance—for example, a pulsating brake pedal or front end shimmy when braking, noisy brakes, or a brake reline that does not last as long as it should have.

Ask the shop owner or mechanic to give you a tour of the shop and show you their equipment. A shop that does tune-up and diagnostic work should have one of the new computerized engine analyzers mentioned above, along with a digital volt/ohmmeter and an exhaust analyzer. If they do electrical work, they should have a volt/ohm/amp tester; a battery charger and load tester; and an alternator/regulator/starter circuit tester.

For brake work, a shop should have a brake drum and disc lathe, dial indicators, and micrometers. For air conditioning work, a gauge set, leak detector, freon recovery and recharging station, and vacuum pump are needed. A shop that does tires, steering, and suspension work should have an alignment rack, a dynamic (spin-type) wheel balancer, and a tire changer.

## CLEAN ORGANIZED SHOP

The repair shop should be reasonably clean and orderly for two reasons. First, mechanics working in a grimy shop tend to leave grease stains inside customers' vehicles, which most people don't appreciate. Second, many repairs require that the vehicle (or part of the vehicle) be disassembled for long periods of time, and if the shop is disorganized, the mechanic may not be able to find some of the parts when he is ready to reassemble the vehicle.

When this happens, the customer is usually told that the repair is going to cost "a little more than we originally thought because another part needs to be replaced."

## CUSTOMER SERVICE

A safe, clean, and comfortable customer waiting area should be provided. All customer service personnel should be knowledgeable and courteous, willing to explain the necessary tests and repairs in language the average person can understand.

169

A signed, written estimate should be required before any work is begun. Customer approval must be obtained for any additional repairs that will exceed the original estimate. All parts installed should be identified by part number and a notation indicating whether they are new, rebuilt or used.

When requested, all replaced parts should be returned to the customer, preferably in the boxes that the new parts came in so the brand names can be checked for quality. The only legitimate excuse for not returning the old parts is to avoid a core charge. If this is the case, the old parts can still be returned if the customer pays the core charge. After examining the old parts to make sure replacement was necessary, the customer can return the parts for a refund or credit.

All repairs should be guaranteed in writing for at least 90 days or 4,000 miles. There should be no parts or labor charges for repairs done under warranty.

# 16

## Secret Warranties:
## How to Get Free Repairs

That's right, *how to get free repairs*. And I don't mean recalls, since most car dealers will gladly tell you if any apply to your car. (So will the manufacturer, if you ask.) In
this chapter, you will learn about several types of secret
warranties that can often be used to get free repairs after
the normal warranty has expired.

Before you ask a dealer or manufacturer if they have
any "secret warranties," you should know that they won't
admit having any. Why not? Because they're against the
law. They might say they have a few "goodwill adjustments," but only a few—and only the ones they want to
do. Most will remain a secret. And the reason they're
called "secret" warranties should be obvious: *They didn't
want you to know.*

## Repair Shop Warranties

Almost all automotive warranties have a time and/or mileage limit, but they are not carved in stone. It is often possible to have repairs done at no charge, or at a greatly reduced charge, even though the written warranty has expired.

A shop owner or service manager may decide to repair a vehicle for free even though the warranty has expired if the vehicle owner is thought of as a valued, long-time customer. When a shop owner or manager says, "Believe me, I really wish I could repair it for free, but the parts are only guaranteed for ninety days, so there's nothing I can do," what he's really saying is that he doesn't see that person as a customer who's valuable enough to bend the rules a little, so he uses the "parts are out of warranty" excuse.

So how can you be thought of as a "valued customer"? By having most (or all) of your repair work done at one shop, so they recognize your name. It also helps to recommend the shop to others—and make sure they mention your name when they bring their vehicle to the shop for the first time. (Obviously, you won't be seen as a valued customer if you're always taking your vehicle to different shops, trying to get the lowest price.)

## Parts Warranties

Technically, most parts do have a specific warranty period, but this is also negotiable between the repair shop and its supplier. The "valued customer" theory also applies to repair shops and their suppliers, so if a shop does a fair amount of business with a parts supplier, they should be able to return parts that went bad within a reasonable time period after the normal warranty runs out.

172

How far out of the normal warranty period the vehicle can be and still be repaired for free depends on how valued the customer is, as well as how much it's going to cost the shop. (This applies to the shop/supplier relationship, too.)

In most cases, a shop can return a defective part and get a free replacement even if it's been six or eight months (or more), so the most they would lose is the labor charge. It's usually a lot easier to negotiate a free repair if it doesn't require a lot of labor to replace the part. If a significant amount of labor is involved, the shop may insist on the customer paying part (or all) of the normal labor charge. (This is especially true if the part lasted well beyond the warranty period.)

So, if a repair needs to be done over within a reasonable time after the "official" warranty has expired, insist on some type of adjustment. For repairs that only last one or two months longer than the warranty, you should be able to get a free repair. If it's been three or four months, you may have to pay something (for example, one-half of the normal charge, or labor only).

Don't accept that old excuse, "I'm sorry, but the parts are only guaranteed for ninety days..." If you hear this, tell them that many shops are willing to extend the warranty a few months because they can exchange the parts with their supplier, then ask them why they can't do the same. If they refuse to make any adjustment, tell them that they are going to lose you as a customer, *then find another shop that has a better warranty policy.*

## Secret Factory Warranties

"Secret factory warranties" provide free repairs for problems that are common to particular makes or models, even though the official factory warranties have run out.

These are known as secret warranties (or "special policy adjustments") because the manufacturers do not publicize them. Vehicle owners are not usually notified that a problem may exist that could be repaired free of charge, even though federal law requires car manufacturers to notify affected consumers and offer free repairs or reimbursement if they've already paid for a covered repair.

Several states have recently passed laws concerning secret warranties that require manufacturers to disclose any special adjustment programs and provide service bulletins describing those programs to consumers. Under the new laws, consumers are also entitled to refunds for covered repairs if they paid for them before the program was announced. (California, Connecticut, Virginia, and Wisconsin currently have state laws on secret warranties.)

Secret warranties normally have a time or mileage limit (usually 1-2 years after the normal warranty has expired), but in some cases free repairs are done with no limitations. At one time, Toyota was replacing exhaust manifolds on certain engines free of charge no matter how many miles were on the cars.

Secret warranties don't usually involve safety problems (for example, possible brake failure, or fuel leaks that could cause a fire). Safety problems almost always trigger factory recalls in which all owners of a particular model receive letters informing them of the problem and asking them to bring in the vehicle for free repairs.

How can consumers find out if their vehicle is covered by any secret warranties? The most reliable way is to send a self-addressed, stamped #10 envelope to the Center for Auto Safety. Here's the address:

Center for Auto Safety
2001 S Street NW, Suite 410
Washington, DC 20009

Include a note listing the year, make, and model of your vehicle, requesting all the information on factory recalls, vehicle defects, and secret warranties. They will then send you, free of charge, whatever information they have on your vehicle. The last time I called the Center, they said they had lists for General Motors, Ford, Chrysler, Toyota, Nissan, Hondas, and a few other makes.

Another (less reliable) method is to call the manufacturer's customer service number and ask if they have any "special warranties" or "goodwill adjustments" that will cover repairs on your vehicle. This number can be found in the vehicle owner's manual and is usually toll free. If you don't have an owner's manual, ask your local dealership for the number.

Consumers can also ask the people working in a local dealership service department if a repair is covered under a "special warranty," but this is not very reliable for the same reason as the above method—secret warranties are illegal, so most car companies won't admit that they exist. Also, most dealership personnel are not told about all of the secret warranties, so even if they wanted to let people know (which some of them don't), they're not able to.

If you ask the dealer or manufacturer, and they offer to fix your vehicle for free without a hassle, consider yourself lucky. If they don't, write the Center for Auto Safety to see if the problem is a common one and whether it's covered by a secret warranty. If it is a common problem, call your manufacturer's customer service number and ask to speak to the district (or zone) manager.

Tell the manager what you received from the Center for Auto Safety, especially if it shows that his company has paid others for the same repair. Ask him if he can get the repairs done under a "special warranty" or "warranty extension." If he says he can't, tell him that you don't think you should have to pay for a major repair so soon

175

after the warranty expired, and that it reflects poorly on his company to have made a vehicle that needs expensive repairs when the mileage is so low.

You can also tell the manager that you know of other car manufacturers (for example, Toyota, Nissan, Honda, etc.) that will repair many items for free even though the official warranty has expired. Tell him that you're going to buy your next car from one of the other companies if you have to pay for the repair.

If you're still not getting anywhere, ask the manager for his name *and* the name and address of the company president. Let him know that you're going to write a letter explaining your situation and the fact that your complaints fell on deaf ears. You can also let him know that you're going to pay another repair shop to do the repairs, then you're going to take the manufacturer to small claims court to get your money back.

Here's one more threat: Tell him that you're going to file a complaint with the Federal Trade Commission. *Then do it.* Manufacturers will often agree to do repairs for free just to keep the FTC out of the picture.

Remember, the law is on your side. Secret warranties are illegal, so the last thing the car companies want to do is have their customers go to the FTC or take them to court. They also don't want to lose customers to their competitors, so make sure you tell them that you're never going to buy one of their cars again if they don't take care of your problem.

**Refunds**

If you didn't know that a particular repair on your vehicle was covered by a secret warranty and you already paid to have the repairs done, you can usually get reimbursed by the manufacturer for the actual cost of repairs. To do this, you need to speak to the district (or zone) manager, and you'll have to go through the same routine mentioned in the previous paragraphs. This procedure has worked for many people, so be persistent.

## How to Get Goodwill Adjustments

If a repair that you need is not on a secret warranty list, that doesn't necessarily mean that you can't get it done for free. Most of the items on the lists were originally covered for one reason—because vehicle owners complained loudly until the repairs were done for free.

When a major part fails within a year or two of the original warranty's expiration, tell them you don't think that part should have failed so soon and you don't think it's fair that you should have to pay for it. Let them know you're not going to give up until they cover the cost of the repair (or at least half of it).

When someone tells you that they can't make any kind of adjustment, ask to speak to their superior. Keep going over their heads until you get results. If you get all the way to the district (or zone) manager and you're told that they're not going to fix it, use the above-mentioned threats about filing a complaint with the FTC and buying your next car from one of their competitors.

It helps to have proof that your particular problem is not unusual. The Center for Auto Safety sometimes has statistics on premature failures, and you can also use factory service bulletins as proof that yours is a common problem that should be repaired for free. For information on obtaining factory service bulletins, see Chapter 14, "Agencies: Who to Call," for the listing of the National Highway Traffic Safety Administration.

The quickest way for consumers to get all of the service bulletins and recalls on their vehicle is to find a repair shop with an Alldata computerized information system. To have this information printed out usually costs about $10 to $15 and can be done in a matter of minutes. To find a shop near you with an Alldata system, call Alldata Corp. at 1-800-829-8727, select "operator."

## NISSAN SECRET WARRANTIES

On June 26, 1990, The Detroit News ran a story on the alleged use of "secret warranties" by Nissan Motor Co. Armed with internal Nissan documents leaked by former Nissan employees, the Center for Auto Safety urged the Federal Trade Commission to investigate.

The internal documents were provided by Fred Gramcko, who was Nissan's U.S. director of consumer support from 1982 to 1989, and by Richard Hoffman, Nissan's U.S. director of engineering from 1979 to 1988. The documents show the amounts paid to dealers by Nissan for out-of-warranty repairs on 1982-87 models.

Nissan denied the charges, claiming that the free repair of some out-of-warranty defects was a "goodwill gesture" by the company, not a secret warranty.

According to the Center for Auto Safety, manufacturers are required by federal law to report any repair frequencies that are above normal for a component and offer free repairs or reimbursement for any past expense.

Offering free repairs (or reimbursement) to some but not all vehicle owners is known as a secret warranty because there is no public announcement or other notification of the defects and many consumers don't realize they are eligible.

In Nissan's case, the defects were not made public and vehicle owners were not notified. The offer of free repairs did not come until after customers had complained.

# Nissan "Secret Warranty" List

## PULSAR, SENTRA
Fuel pump assembly -- 1983-85.
Vacuum control modulator -- 1984-86.
Rear suspension -- 1984-87.

## 200SX
Rear spring -- 1986.
Front door finisher -- 1985.

## STANZA
Carburetor assembly -- 1983.
Torque converter -- 1984.
Transmission case -- 1983.

## STANZA WAGON
Governor assembly -- 1986.
Steering gear rack -- 1986-87.

## ZX
Turbocharger -- 1986.
Battery heat shield -- 1985-86.
ATC control assembly -- 1983.
Exhaust gas warning system -- 1985.

## TRUCK
Cylinder block -- 1984.
Cylinder head gasket -- 1982.
Transmission case -- 1986.

## MAXIMA
Drive plate assembly -- 1986.
Muffler -- 1986.
Alternator -- 1985-86.

Starter -- 1987.
Battery -- 1985.
Head lamp -- 1986.
Fuel level sensor -- 1986.
Compressor assembly -- 1984-85.
Antenna -- 1985-86.
Torque converter -- 1985-87.
Transmission case -- 1986.
Oil pump -- 1985.
Clutch assembly -- 1986.
Sunroof motor -- 1986.
Steering gear -- 1985-87.

# TOYOTA SECRET WARRANTIES

On August 26, 1988, The Detroit News ran a story revealing that Toyota Motor Corp. will sometimes offer free out-of-warranty repairs, but only if people ask for them.

A twelve-page Toyota document was leaked anonymously to The News, using company stationery from Toyota's Cincinnati distributor. The document lists 41 components on certain models that Toyota has repaired for free after the warranty has expired.

Bob Daly, Toyota's national service operations manager, confirmed the authenticity of the document, but added that customers usually have to complain about paying for an item that is on the "high frequency of repair" list before the company will offer reimbursement.

Daly also stated that those repairs were done under the company's customer satisfaction policy, and were not examples of secret warranties.

Upon examination of the Toyota repairs list, the Center for Auto Safety claimed that it "clearly constitutes a secret warranty."

# Toyota "Secret Warranty" List

1. Oil filter damage -- 1983 Corollas & Tercels.
2. Camshaft -- Supras & Cressidas.
3. Catalytic convertors -- some light trucks.
4. Cruise control (actuator accelerating) --
                            all models, all years.
5. Dashboard pads (cracks, warping) --
                            all models, all years.
6. Disc rotors (rust, flaking) -- 1983-86 Tercels.
7. Exhaust manifolds.
8. Exhaust shields.
9. Fuel pumps -- cars only, all years.
10. Fuel tanks (external rust) -- all models, all years.
11. Oil consumption -- all years.
12. Paint peeling (blue only) -- trucks thru 1984.
13. Power train-related -- all 1983-86 models.
14. Rust perforation -- all models thru 1986.
15. Seat back, seat track (bent, warped, deformed) --
                            1982 Tercels.
16. Shock absorbers -- some trucks.
17. Speedometer shaft sleeve (oil leak) --
                            all models, all years.
18. Thrust washer -- 1983 Celicas, some '83 trucks.
19. Transmission front input shaft bearing (L-52
        transmission only) -- four 1981-83 truck models.
20. Universal steering joint -- eight Tercel models.
21. Water pumps -- 1983-84 Camrys.
22. Rear wheel bearings -- 1981-83 Tercels.
23. Rocker arm wear (22-R engine only) --
                            1983-84 Celicas & trucks.
24. Truck engines (cylinder wear).
25. Muffler corrosion (loud noise or separation at
                        front pipe) -- Camrys.
26. Horn terminal rust -- some Celicas & Corollas.

27. Paint peeling -- some 1983 Supras,
    some 1983-84 trucks.
28. Oil sending unit -- Celicas (1983-84 only), vans,
    trucks, Corollas, Supras, Cressidas.
29. Oil pump gaskets -- Camrys.
30. Front disc brake vibration -- some Camry SV &
    CV models.
31. Automatic transmission (slippage) -- 1983 Camry SV,
    1984 Camry CV, 1985 Corolla CE.
32. Air conditioner compressor lock sensors -- Camrys.
33. Diesel cylinder head gaskets -- Camrys.
34. Lower arm bushing separation -- 1984-86 Camrys.
35. Sulfur odor -- 1984-86 Camrys, Celicas, Tercels.
36. Engine won't start on hill -- 1985-86 Camry SV.
37. Sun roof computer -- 1984-85 Cressidas.
38. Head gaskets -- 1985-86 trucks, 1985 Celicas.
39. Crankshaft and pulley -- vans thru July 1985.
40. Power steering gear-box oil leak -- all Cressidas.
41. Radiator fan motors -- 1983-86 Tercels.

**Note:** These articles and lists were only included to illustrate how many secret warranties may exist at any one time, so be sure to send for current information.

Make sure you send for the lists of defects and secret warranty items for *all* the vehicles you've owned for the last two or three years—you may be entitled to a refund for repairs that were done in the past.

# 17

# Vehicle Maintenance "Secrets"

Would you like to get 100,000 miles or more out of your vehicles without experiencing (or at least paying for) any major engine or transmission repairs? Well, between secret warranties and proper maintenance, that is very possible to do on most vehicles. Keep reading and you'll learn how to do just that.

The first "secret" is: *Read the Owner's Manual!* This shouldn't be a secret, but many people don't read and follow the maintenance schedule in their owner's manual, then they complain when they have to pay for major repairs because their car wasn't properly maintained.

For those of you who claim that you can't remember to perform scheduled maintenance on your vehicle, try writing yourself notes such as, "change oil" or "tune-up" on your calendar where you estimate the work should be done based on time or mileage. Also, go to a stationery store and buy an auto record book to record the date and mileage of all maintenance work and repairs.

If you bought a used vehicle and the owner's manual is missing, ask a local dealership who sells that type of vehicle where you might find one; if that doesn't work, go to a library, bookstore or major magazine distributor to look at the classified ads in several auto magazines. There are many car clubs and collectors of old manuals who would probably have the one you are looking for.

The second "secret" is: *Never* drive your vehicle when it's really low on oil or water, or when the engine temperature or oil pressure gauges read in the danger zone (indicating an overheating or low oil pressure condition). As a mechanic, I have seen hundreds of blown-up engines, and almost all of them were out of water or oil (or both).

Even if your engine doesn't blow up immediately after it's driven without oil or water, it will have already suffered serious damage, drastically reducing its useful life span. This is why some people end up paying for an engine overhaul at 75,000 miles or less while others (whose cars never ran out of oil or water) are still driving around with the original engine at 150,000 miles.

If you are driving your vehicle and the temperature gauge suddenly drops to the "cold" side, pull over as quickly as possible and check the coolant level in the radiator—all of the coolant may have just leaked out.

On some vehicles, it's possible to overheat the engine without it registering on the temperature gauge if all of the coolant suddenly leaks out. This can happen if the temperature sending unit needs to be immersed in liquid to measure the coolant temperature (which is a rather poor design, I might add).

The third "secret" is that there are no short-cuts for properly maintaining a vehicle, but the end results are definitely worth the effort. For example, I have seen many automatic transmissions that lasted at least 130,000 miles without any major repairs because the fluid was changed every 30,000 miles. I have also seen many transmissions that needed overhauls at only 70,000 miles because they had never been serviced. Regular, inexpensive maintenance can double the life of an expensive transmission.

It's always easier (and less expensive) to have a vehicle worked on at your convenience than it is to wait until it breaks down, which can result in a towing bill and serious engine or transmission damage. Since many parts on a vehicle will not last forever, replacing them near the end of their expected life span can prevent the inconvenience and expense of a breakdown.

For example, if you live in an area that has cold winters and your four-year battery is almost four years old in the fall, replacing it before winter arrives would be a wise thing to do since the odds are that the battery would not make it through the winter, anyway.

As a general rule, you should follow the manufacturer's recommendations listed in the maintenance schedule of your owner's manual, with one possible exception: fluid changes. Most professional technicians recommend more frequent changes for motor oil and transmission/ differential fluids.

Pay particular attention to the manufacturer's description of "severe operating conditions," as these call for more frequent service. Towing a trailer; driving on rough, dusty, or muddy roads; driving in severe hot or cold weather; frequent stop-and-go driving; and repeated short distance driving are all considered to be severe conditions.

If you're tempted to scrimp on frequent oil and other fluid changes because you don't think the manufacturer requires them, remember these two things: First, the factory warranties only cover engines and transmissions for the first 3 or 4 years. And second, car companies are in the business of selling as many *new* vehicles as possible, so there's no incentive for them to help people get 100,000 miles or more out of their vehicles.

## Checking Under the Hood

The oil and coolant levels should be checked at every other fuel fill-up (or two weeks). Add fluids if necessary; check for leaks if any fluid levels are low and repair as needed. *Keep an eye on the oil level*—don't let it drop below the "add" line, or serious engine damage may result. If the engine leaks or burns oil, check it frequently— every day, if necessary. (Yes, I know this is inconvenient, but not as much as an engine that blew up because it ran out of oil.)

If your vehicle has an automatic transmission, check its fluid level once a month. Watch for fluid discoloration or a burnt odor, as these are usually signs of transmission overheating or internal problems. Service if necessary.

Other items that should be checked once a month include the drive belts and coolant hoses, the brake fluid level, and (if equipped) the power steering and clutch cylinder fluid levels.

Check the air filter every 2 to 3 months and replace if necessary. Depending on driving conditions, air filters usually last at least 10,000 miles before they need to be replaced.

## Lube, Oil & Filter Change

Most of the vehicle manufacturers recommend a lube, oil and filter change every 7,500 miles under "normal" driving conditions. However, they also recommend more frequent changes under "severe" conditions like frequent stop-and-go driving and/or repeated short distance driving, so most motorists should probably be following the schedule for severe conditions.

A lube, oil and filter change should be done *at least* every 4,000 to 5,000 miles (or 4 to 5 months) under normal conditions, and 3,000 to 4,000 miles (3 to 4 months) under severe conditions. And make sure the oil filter is changed with the oil, or a quart of dirty oil will be left in the engine.

Use only high-quality, name-brand filters and oil. It's not worth risking an engine to save a few dollars buying inexpensive parts. (Many of the cheaper filters do not filter the oil as well as the name-brand ones.) Follow the manufacturer's recommendations for oil type and grade.

**Cooling System Service**

The cooling system is often neglected by vehicle owners until their vehicle overheats; unfortunately, by the time a driver notices that something is wrong, the engine may already be seriously damaged. As a mechanic, I have seen hundreds of engines that had to be replaced because they were driven while they were overheated. To prevent this from happening to you, make sure that the cooling system is in good condition and that it always has the proper coolant level.

Most radiator hoses, heater hoses and drive belts have an average life span of about 3 to 4 years, so it's a good idea to have them inspected when they're 3 years old to see if they need replacement. (This may be necessary every 2 to 3 years under extreme conditions, such as prolonged hot weather or towing a trailer.)

If one hose (or belt) fails and all of the rest are at least 3 years old, replace all of them at the same time. This will prevent repeated changing of the hoses or belts, one at a time, as they fail. After replacing the drive belts, put the old ones in the trunk. (They might be needed someday as emergency replacements if you have car trouble out on the highway.)

The recommended interval for flushing the radiator and replacing the coolant is every 2 to 3 years (depending on driving conditions), so make sure this is done at the same time the radiator and heater hoses are replaced to save money.

If you see any drops or puddles of coolant on the ground where your vehicle is parked, open the hood and check the coolant level in the recovery bottle and radiator. *Never remove the radiator cap on a hot engine,* or you may end up in the burn ward at your local hospital.

Before removing the radiator cap, squeeze the upper radiator hose to make sure the engine has cooled and the system is not under pressure. If the hose feels hot and "inflated," don't remove the cap yet; the system is still under pressure. Wait until the hose feels cool and not "inflated" anymore, then slowly turn the radiator cap (counterclockwise), pausing at the safety notch to release any residual pressure before removing the cap completely.

Almost all manufacturers recommend checking the coolant level in the plastic coolant recovery bottle instead of taking the radiator cap off and checking the level in the radiator. (They usually say not to remove the radiator cap at all, but to check and add all coolant at the recovery bottle.)

There are two reasons for this recommendation: The first is that a properly operating cooling system (with no leaks and a good radiator cap) will have a full radiator when the level in the coolant recovery bottle is correct. The second reason is safety—a person can be severely burned removing a radiator cap on a hot engine if they don't know what they are doing.

However, failure to check the coolant level in the radiator can result in overheating and serious engine damage if the cooling system develops a leak or the radiator cap fails to work properly. When this happens, there will not be any suction to draw the coolant out of the recovery bottle and into the radiator, resulting in an empty radiator even though the recovery bottle is full. *Don't assume that the radiator level is all right just because the coolant recovery bottle is full.*

Checking the levels in the radiator and the recovery bottle is also a good way to tell whether the cooling system is sealed properly. If the radiator level has dropped, but the level in the recovery bottle has not, the system should be tested for leaks or a defective radiator cap.

## Tires

Tire pressures should be checked regularly, making sure they are fully inflated when cold. Under-inflation by as little as 2 to 3 lbs. will not only reduce the life of the tire, but will also increase fuel consumption and affect vehicle handling.

Check your owner's manual or call a tire dealer for the correct tire pressure for your vehicle. (The pressure that is listed on the side of the tire is the *maximum* tire pressure, beyond which the tire may blow out if driven at high speeds for an extended period of time. This is not usually the correct pressure for that tire on your vehicle.)

If most of your driving is done at freeway speeds, add 2 lbs. to the recommended tire pressure, but *do not* exceed the maximum pressure listed on the side of the tire.

To extend the life of your tires, have them rotated (from front to rear only) every 6,000 miles. Have this done at the same time as a lube, oil, and filter change to save money. (If your vehicle is already up on a hoist for an oil change, the charge for a tire rotation should only be a fraction of the normal price.)

While they are rotating the tires, have them check the brakes. It only takes a minute to check the brakes when the wheels are already off, so there shouldn't be an extra charge for this. Ask the mechanic how the tires look and whether they indicate the need for any adjustments or repairs (for example, shock absorbers or alignment).

Whenever new tires are installed on the front of a vehicle, the front end should be checked for worn parts, and the alignment should be checked and adjusted if necessary. If this is not done, uneven tire wear may result, shortening the useful life of the tires.

**Annual (Safety) Inspection**

To prevent unnecessary breakdowns, and to catch problems before they become major ones, have your mechanic inspect your vehicle once a year. (You can save money by having this done at the same time as an oil change, tire rotation, and brake inspection, since many items would be checked anyway as a part of those services.)

The purpose of this inspection is to visually check all mechanical and electrical systems on a vehicle for any signs of potential problems such as cracked brake hoses, fluid leaks, rust holes in the exhaust system, leaking or worn shock absorbers, unusual tire wear, worn front end parts, corrosion build-up on battery terminals, frayed electrical wires, burnt transmission fluid, etc.

A visual inspection of this type should only take about 30 minutes, so the cost should be about $30 or less. If a serious problem is discovered, more time may be required for disassembly and diagnosis, but you can tell the shop not to spend more than 30 minutes on the inspection without calling you for approval.

## Engine Tune-up

Due to improvements in automotive technology, today's vehicles require fewer engine tune-ups than those built before the 1980s. And when a tune-up is done, fewer parts need to be changed. There are no more points and condensers to replace due to widespread use of electronic ignition, and improvements in distributor cap design have generally eliminated the need to replace them with every tune-up. (Some models don't even have a distributor; if that's the case on your vehicle, there will be no rotor or cap to replace.)

Most late-model vehicles can usually go at least 30,000 miles between minor tune-ups. Use the recommended interval for spark plug replacement found in your owner's manual (it's usually 30,000 miles), and perform the other related services at the same time.

A minor tune-up should include replacement of the spark plugs, fuel filter, rotor (if equipped), and cleaning or replacing the PCV valve. The distributor cap (if equipped), spark plug wires, air filter, and breather element should be checked and replaced if necessary. Insist on the use of high-quality, name-brand parts.

After all necessary parts have been replaced, the engine should be tested on an analyzer to make sure no other problems exist and to adjust the timing, idle speed and air/fuel ratio (if possible).

Remember, *a tune-up will not cure all driveability problems.* If your engine is running rough, don't ask the repair shop to give it a tune-up; tell them it's running rough and you want them to diagnose the problem before you agree to any repairs. Your vehicle may only need a $7 spark plug wire, or it may need major engine work that a tune-up wouldn't cover. In either case, getting a tune-up would be a waste of time and money.

## Valve Adjustment

Most four cylinder (and some six cylinder) engines have adjustable valves that should be inspected periodically and adjusted if necessary. Failure to have this done can result in burnt valves, which means that the engine will need a valve job costing $600 to $800 (or more).

Recommended intervals for this service vary from one car manufacturer to the next (most are around 30,000 miles), so be sure to check your owner's manual for the correct interval.

## Automatic Transmission Service

Automatic transmissions should be serviced at least every 30,000 miles (15,000 miles if the vehicle is used to pull a trailer). The service should include draining and refilling the transmission, new fluid, a new filter, band adjustment (if applicable), and a visual inspection for leaks or other potential problems.

Watch for transmission fluid leaks; repair them before they become a major problem. If the fluid level gets too low, the transmission may slip in and out of gear, or it may not go into gear at all. Transmission damage may result if the vehicle is operated when the fluid is low.

## Manual Transmission/Transaxle Service

Change the fluid in a manual transmission or transaxle at 50,000 mile intervals, more often if recommended by the manufacturer or the vehicle is used to pull a trailer. Check the fluid level and inspect for leaks at every oil change. Repair any leaks as soon as they are discovered, because operating the vehicle without fluid will quickly destroy the transmission or transaxle.

The clutch adjustment should be checked every 7,500 miles/6 months under normal conditions, or 3,000 miles/3 months if the vehicle is operated under severe conditions. Adjust if necessary to maintain proper free-play (usually at least 3/8-1/2"). Failure to maintain proper free-play can cause premature clutch failure.

**Differential Service**

Change the fluid in a differential at 50,000 mile intervals, more often if recommended by the manufacturer or the vehicle is used to pull a trailer. On some vehicles, it may not be possible to drain the differential without major disassembly. If this is the case, use a siphoning device to remove as much fluid as possible through the fill hole, then refill the differential with new fluid.

Check the fluid level and inspect for leaks at every oil change. Repair any leaks as soon as they are discovered; operating the vehicle without fluid will quickly destroy the differential.

**Air Conditioning**

Routine servicing of the air conditioning system is not usually necessary. If a large amount of bugs and/or leaves becomes stuck in the condenser (in front of the radiator), they should be blown out with compressed air.

Be sure to run the air conditioner for several minutes at least once a week, especially during the winter when it normally wouldn't be used for months. It needs to be run periodically to keep the seals from drying out and to lubricate other internal parts. Failure to do this can result in major repair bills to restore the air conditioning system.

Repair any leaks as soon as they are discovered, because the oil in the system leaks out along with the refrigerant. If too much oil leaks out and the system is run, the compressor will be damaged.

## Timing Belts

For vehicles equipped with rubber timing belts (mostly 4 cylinder engines), most manufacturers recommend replacement at 60,000 miles (a few say 90,000). Be sure to check your manual for the proper mileage interval; if the recommendation isn't there, replace the belt anyway. This item is extremely important—failure to replace the timing belt when recommended can result in major towing and repair bills if the belt breaks when the engine is running.

## SUMMARY

Regular maintenance and periodic inspections can prevent the need for most major repairs. And maintaining the proper fluid levels is crucial, so watch the ground under your car for signs of fluid leaks and check the levels if you notice anything unusual.

Finally, you don't have to use a dealership for scheduled maintenance to keep your warranty in effect; any qualified repair shop can do the work (and probably for less money). All that's needed to maintain the warranty is to have copies of repair orders showing that the maintenance was done.

# 18

# Are Chain Stores Cleaning Up Their Act?

The big Sears scandal in 1992 was followed by similar charges of fraudulent repair practices at a number of other well-known chains. Most were caught selling unnecessary repairs during undercover investigations that were conducted by state regulators, and a few were caught by TV crews using hidden cameras. Some were also caught using the same type of sales commissions, contests and/or quotas that got Sears in trouble.

Those investigations led to several major events: a Senate subcommittee hearing on auto repair fraud, an auto repair task force made up of state prosecutors, and the creation of a new repair industry coalition.

Because of the Sears bust and statements that were made regarding the use of "common practices" like sales incentive programs and replacing parts before they fail, the U.S. Senate called a subcommittee hearing to look into the repair practices of chain stores.

At the 1992 hearing, the Maryland Attorney General called for an amendment to a federal law to make franchisers legally responsible for deceptive or fraudulent practices by their franchisees. He said auto repair franchisers have no economic incentive to discourage fraudulent practices because franchisers profit from all business activity at their stores, whether they're honest or not.

Other reform proposals presented at the hearing included licensing of repair shops, setting minimum standards for certification of mechanics, holding parent companies to strict standards of liability, and eliminating the commission-based sales structure.

Commission-based sales was listed as a problem area because Sears was using it to determine the earnings of its service advisors. Goodyear (and others) were also found to be using commissions after their shops were caught selling unnecessary repairs during undercover investigations.

## NAAG AUTO REPAIR TASK FORCE

Another outcome of the Sears scandal was creation of the National Association of Attorneys General (NAAG) Auto Repair Task Force, which was set up to protect consumers and address problem areas in the repair industry. The task force conducted a broad-based study of repair shop practices, especially in the areas of ethics, lack of training (incompetence), and commission-based pay for mechanics and service advisors. In October of 1995, the Task Force released its findings in a 139-page report.

The Task Force Report said that consumer complaints are usually due to the "Four C's": *communication* (lack of communication between technicians and customers), *competence* (inadequate training, lack of continuing education, and lack of proper equipment), *complexity* (technological advances and design changes in vehicles), and *consumer fraud* (fraudulent, unfair or deceptive business practices).

Their report also said that fraud, technician error and incompetence were responsible for many unnecessary repairs, adding that compensation programs for mechanics still play a big part in auto repair fraud. The report suggests that repair shops avoid using commissions, bonuses, contests and quotas based on sales. It suggested using rewards based on customer satisfaction, productivity, quality of repairs and advanced training.

## MOTORIST ASSURANCE PROGRAM
### (The Chain Stores' Solution)

Charges of fraudulent repair practices at Sears sent shock waves throughout the whole industry in 1992. Auto service sales at Sears fell 23% after the scandal hit the news, and business also dropped off at other repair shops across the country. Consumers' distrust of the repair industry had become so bad that many people were putting off basic auto maintenance and service out of fear that they might get ripped off.

To improve consumer confidence in the industry after the Sears scandal, the Automotive Parts & Accessories Association (APAA) and Sears created "MAP," the Motorist Assurance Program. (The original title was "Maintenance Awareness Program," which revealed their true motivation: selling people a lot of maintenance and repairs. That was a flop, so the title was quickly changed to the newer, more consumer-friendly one.)

The initial members of MAP were mostly chain stores and their parts manufacturers, but the group eventually grew to include a majority of the nation's multi-bay retail automotive outlets (i.e., chain stores), suppliers, manufacturers, industry associations and publications. MAP now promotes itself as "an industry-wide coalition."

Initial goals of MAP included developing uniform inspection procedures, a code of ethics, standards of service, and preventive maintenance recommendations. Long-term goals included upgrading the skill levels of technicians and service writers, improving the public image of professional technicians, and giving recognition to outstanding individuals.

Contained in the code of ethics developed by MAP are requirements that repair shops: 1) recommend service based on system failure, preventive maintenance, or improved performance, and clearly explain service needs to the consumer; 2) provide a written estimate and not perform any work without the customer's permission; 3) train and hire qualified personnel; and 4) include a written, limited warranty at no charge.

**Were Chain Stores Sincere About Reform?**

The MAP goals and promises *sound* good. After all, who could argue with having ethical standards, written estimates, warranties and inspection guidelines? And most MAP members are no doubt sincere about setting high ethical standards and implementing them, because they've had them all along. (The ones who haven't been busted, anyway.)

However, the driving force behind MAP was (and still is) the large chain operations, as well as the parts manufacturers and suppliers who benefit from the chains' massive sales of parts. And the biggest players in MAP are the chains that have been in trouble.

Because these companies are all in business to make money by selling tons of parts, it's only prudent to be a little suspicious of the chains' claim that they're cleaning up their act. After all, selling a lot of unnecessary repairs has always been very profitable for them.

I decided to take a close look at exactly what MAP and the chains *said* they were going to do, as well as what they've actually done. The following sections summarize what I have found. (References to MAP policies and goals came from their own published materials and from an interview with MAP President Larry Hecker that was broadcast on KGO-TV in late 1997.)

## What MAP (and the Chains) Really Said

First, MAP's stated objective has always been "to improve the image of the industry" and "to restore customer trust and confidence." They never said that they were going to clean up the industry by getting rid of commissions, contests and quotas (or even deceptive ads).

Their own "Fact Sheet for Consumer Advocates" said, "MAP isn't some kind of PR ploy meant to paper over problems and get the customer to 'feel good' about shops." However, if those offending practices are not eliminated, many chain stores will continue to sell parts and services that aren't necessary—and MAP will, in fact, be nothing more than a PR ploy for chains.

MAP also describes itself as "a unique, powerful and proactive program of self-regulation," adding that "The choice is simple: Regulate ourselves...or face unwanted government regulations." MAP's material also says that the group was formed "to deal with adverse media reports and government/regulatory activity."

So, first and foremost, MAP is a group that represents the interests of the repair industry, not the consumer. In fact, MAP's president said, "I wouldn't call it a consumer-protection program. I consider it more of a communications program..."

## Chain Store Scam #1: "Self-Regulation"

With the chains' track record of fraud (some going back over 20 years), and their obvious motive for continuing it (higher profits), most people would have serious doubts about their claims of reform. And fewer still would believe that they could be trusted to "self-regulate."

However, through MAP, the chains have succeeded in surrounding themselves with scores of reputable automotive companies, giving some chains the appearance of respectability that they don't deserve. If their intent in building a huge coalition was to fool people by "getting lost in the crowd," they might have succeeded—temporarily.

Remember, MAP said, "Regulate ourselves...or face unwanted government regulations." They were tired of all the undercover busts and the bad publicity (it hurts their sales), so they set out to convince state regulators that they could be trusted to regulate (or police) themselves.

MAP's newsletter said, "We are campaigning for...an opportunity to handle the complaints the state gets....In California, we formed an alliance with the Automotive Repair Coalition to work on the Sunset Review of the California Bureau of Automotive Repair (or BAR)."

If the chains succeed in handling all of the complaints against their own shops, that will probably mean the end of all state enforcement actions against them. Why? Because the states won't know the type and volume of complaints, and that is what initiates undercover stings.

## Chain Store Scam #2: "We're Innocent—Our Mechanics Are Responsible"

Chains have several tricks that they use to avoid blame when their shops are caught selling unnecessary repairs. The "CYA" document is a common one: Employees are forced to sign a document that says, "I understand that it is against company policy to recommend or sell repairs that are not necessary." Then, after signing that document, employees are taught to sell unnecessary repairs or they're put to work in an environment of commissions, contests or quotas that encourages massive (and often deceptive) sales of parts and services.

Another common trick is the "incompetence" excuse. Many chain stores intentionally avoid hiring the best mechanics they can find for several reasons: First, highly skilled mechanics cost more money—and they sell fewer parts (assuming they're honest). Unskilled workers are a lot cheaper, and it's a lot easier to train them to sell a lot of parts that may not be necessary.

If a company is using both of these tricks and they're caught in an undercover sting, all they have to say is "It's the mechanics' fault. See this document? Selling unnecessary repairs is against company policy, and they knew it because they signed right here. I guess they were just incompetent." *And those excuses have been used for years.*

## Chain Store Scam #3:
## "Recommended/Suggested Repairs"

To avoid charges of fraud by state regulators, many chain stores have been using the terms "recommended" or "suggested" when selling unnecessary repairs. (That's still deceptive if they fail to tell people that the repairs are not needed or required according to industry standards.)

Shops belonging to MAP have been caught doing this in undercover investigations. And they've been caught telling customers (verbally) that repairs were "needed," and changing the repair order to reflect a "recommended/preventive maintenance" repair. Some have refused to do routine brake jobs without replacing other expensive parts, telling customers that the shop can't guarantee the brakes unless the additional parts are replaced.

## Were State Regulators Fooled, or Double-Crossed?

The prosecutors' Task Force correctly identified the problems caused by sales commissions, contests and quotas, and recommended that those practices be eliminated. And the final report of the Task Force said that "any code of ethics should include...as minimum standards, the Task Force recommendations...to ensure that industry self-regulation will adequately protect and benefit consumers."

However, MAP has not promised (or attempted) to end the use of commissions, contests or quotas, nor has it included the elimination of those offensive practices in its code of ethics. As their president said (in his description of MAP), "I wouldn't call it a consumer-protection program. I consider it more of a communications program so that consumers can...be able to make the right decisions." *And it's probably safe to assume that the "right decisions" will involve more profitable repairs.*

Task Force members were told that MAP would create written guidelines that shops would use to perform inspections and to determine what repairs (if any) were needed, and that MAP members would follow those guidelines. Several experts who have examined MAP's Uniform Inspection Guidelines said that they appear to be a justification for the way that mass merchandisers (chains) want to repair cars: focusing on parts replacement instead of repair. Why? Because of higher profits.

Recent undercover investigations found that many chain stores are not using the MAP guidelines. Worse yet, MAP (and its members) are now saying that their own "Uniform Inspection Guidelines" were *not* designed for their mechanics to perform inspections. MAP's president said the guidelines were "designed as a communications tool...so that the motorist can understand what their vehicle needs..." *So the guidelines will be used as sales tools, not standards for inspections or repairs.*

After a wave of state enforcement actions against chain stores from 1992 to 1995, things were relatively quiet. Quiet for the big-name MAP members, anyway. California busted about 60 (smaller) chain stores that were not in MAP, and only 5 shops that were. (In the previous 3-year period, about 60 big-name shops were busted in California.)

Was the drastic reduction in big-name busts proof that the chains were cleaning up their act? Well, several recent undercover investigations show that too many were still up to their old tricks. Only this time, most of the investigations were done by TV stations.

If it was so easy for the TV crews to find auto repair rip-offs at big-name companies, why weren't the state regulators doing investigations? Did they stop because the chains convinced them that the rip-offs had ended? And finally, since rip-offs were still occurring, were the regulators fooled, or double-crossed by the chains?

In California, the top auto repair regulator is the chief of the Bureau of Automotive Repair, who is appointed by the governor. The current Bureau chief has been there since 1995 and his term will probably end in early 1999 when the new governor arrives.

Recent events seem to indicate that the BAR chief may have been fooled by the chains. In 1998, the BAR released its report on problem areas in that state's auto repair market. In spite of input from the industry (and its own experts) that deceptive practices were still serious problems, the final report said that incompetent mechanics were the biggest problem and fraud was only a minor element. Sales commissions, contests and quotas were not identified as problem areas by the Bureau. The report also said, "Some industry leaders stated that mass merchandisers express concern about doing business in California largely because of the Bureau's enforcement actions."

Then, in 1998, KCBS conducted a huge undercover investigation that found fraud in dozens of chain stores in the LA area. State legislators held a hearing on the results of that sting, and the BAR chief was asked to explain why his agency had not been investigating those chains. He said the BAR had been focusing on auto body and transmission shops for the last three years, and they didn't have the resources to investigate the chains, too.

It's ironic that the chief of the most respected auto repair regulator in the country would end up being embarrassed by a huge chain store sting in his own back yard. Especially when the career enforcement staff of his own agency knew all about the chains—because they had been busting them for years. *Maybe the Bureau chief should have listened to his own experts.*

### Recent Investigations

Shops from four of the biggest chains were caught recommending and/or selling unnecessary repairs between 1995 and 1998. (All were MAP members.) California's BAR caught 8 Goodyear shops in 1995, 4 Midas Muffler shops between 1996 and 1997, and 1 Aamco shop in 1998.

KSTP-TV (St. Paul, MN) caught 4 Firestone stores in 1996. The big KCBS-TV investigation in Southern California caught 4 Midas Muffler shops, 6 Montgomery Ward shops, plus dozens of other chain stores in 1998.

When a chain store executive was asked to explain the massive fraud that was found by KCBS, he used the chains' favorite excuse: *He blamed it on the mechanics.*

# Summary

After reading this book, some might say that I painted a rather dark picture of chain stores. But I have to admit, I couldn't have done it without their help. If it wasn't for all their undercover busts (and their dirty little secrets), I wouldn't have had much to write about.

And I hope this book didn't leave the impression that people will get ripped off no matter where they go, because I don't believe that's true. There are many honest, professional repair shops in the country, but consumers must learn how to find them because they're not as visible as the ones that do a lot of advertising.

Speaking of honest shops, I found a great tire company a few years ago. I checked them out thoroughly (OK, I spied on them) and was surprised to discover that there was actually a large chain of tire stores with a spotless reputation. Besides being the most honest people you'll ever find in the business, they also promise to beat their competitors' prices on name-brand tires. In Oregon and Northern California, they're known as "America's Tire Co." In Southern California and 11 other states, they're known as "Discount Tire Co."

Now that you know where to buy tires, you may still need an honest repair shop. Use the guidelines in this book to find a reputable shop that employs well-trained, highly skilled technicians who aren't working with sales commissions or quotas. The best place to look is usually in large, independent repair shops.

Advice on oil changes: If you insist on using one of those "fast and cheap" oil change places, think of it as "fast food for your car." It probably won't hurt to do it once in a while, but you wouldn't want to make a steady diet of it. Why not? Because your vehicle needs maintenance and inspections that those places can't handle.

Remember these tips:

- Check out a shop and its mechanics *before* taking your vehicle in for repairs.
- Get a detailed, written estimate before any work is started. Make sure the problem or symptom that you want diagnosed/repaired is written on the original estimate.
- If a shop says a repair is "needed," tell them to put it in writing *before* you authorize the repair. If they won't do that, you probably don't need it.
- If a shop says a repair is "recommended" or "suggested" because of mileage (or as preventive maintenance), that means you don't need it immediately. And it means that you have time to get a second opinion.
- Request that all replaced parts be returned to you.
- For major repairs, always get a second (or third) opinion before authorizing any work.

## Car News & Secrets On the Internet

Make sure you visit "CarInfo.com" (www.carinfo.com) for the latest consumer protection information on cars. This Web site covers new-car buying and leasing secrets, and it even has worksheets to figure out if you were cheated on a lease. Tell your friends about it!